THE JEWISH PERSPECTIVES SERIES
OF THE HEBREW UNION COLLEGE PRESS

The Jewish Perspectives series
presents scholarly works that are
of broad interest and relevant to
contemporary Jewish life.

EUGENE MIHALY
A Song to Creation: A Dialogue with a Text

SHELDON H. BLANK
Prophetic Thought: Essays and Addresses

HAROLD M. SCHULWEIS
Evil and the Morality of God

SANDRA B. LUBARSKY
*Tolerance and Transformation:
Jewish Approaches to Religious Pluralism*

Tolerance
and
Transformation
Jewish Approaches to
Religious Pluralism

SANDRA B. LUBARSKY

HEBREW UNION COLLEGE PRESS
Cincinnati

Library of Congress Cataloging-in-Publication Data

Lubarsky, Sandra B.
    Tolerance and transformation : Jewish approaches to religious pluralism /
by Sandra B. Lubarsky.
        p. cm. — (Jewish perspectives ; 4)
    Includes bibliographical references.
    ISBN 0-87820-504-7
    1. Judaism — Relations — Christianity. 2. Christianity and other
religions — Judaism. 3. Judaism — 20th century. 4. Dialogue —
Religious aspects. 5. Religious pluralism. I. Title.
II. Series.
BM535.L76 1990
296.3'872 — dc20   90-4206
                                                                         CIP

Printed on acid-free paper
Manufactured in the United States of America
Distributed by Behrman House, Inc.
235 Watchung Avenue, West Orange, New Jersey 07052

This book is dedicated to my husband,
Marcus Peter Ford

Contents

Acknowledgments

This book began as an inquiry into the meaning of chosenness in a pluralistic world. Very soon into that project, the issue of competing truth claims became central, and I was led into the larger world of comparative religions and from there into interreligious dialogue. In this pluralistic society, it seems not only pretentious but also anachronistic to try to make sense of (or to declare as nonsense) the idea of chosenness without reference to the self-understandings of other traditions. It has become clear to me that dialogue between traditions is fundamental to doing theology.

I am particularly indebted to two individuals for their guidance and encouragement on this project. Professor John B. Cobb, Jr., both before and since serving as my dissertation advisor, has been my "master teacher." It has been my great good luck to study with him; his book, *Beyond Dialogue: Toward a Mutual Transformation of Christianity and Buddhism,* has been my model for this study.

When I began my doctoral studies, David Ellenson's course in modern Jewish thought at the Hebrew Union College, Los Angeles, electrified me. He has continued to be a source of knowledge and encouragement, and I have been sustained by his friendship.

I am grateful to Eureka College, Eureka, Illinois, which provided me with funds for this project. In particular, I want to thank the library staff which, under the direction of Ms. Nancy Blomstrom, provided me with extensive interlibrary loans and endless renewals.

Professor Michael A. Meyer and his assistants, Ms. Barbara Selya and Rabbi Faedra Lazar Weiss, read the entire manuscript and offered many helpful suggestions on both style and content.

I am thankful, too, for the many years of support and encouragement given to me by my parents—Ruth Lubarsky, Barbara Ford, and Dr. Peter Ford.

This book is dedicated to my husband, Marcus Peter Ford. Many times our mutual students have wondered what our dinner conversations are like: over the past five years they very often have been about this manuscript. Marcus' unwavering support, his critical remarks and leading insights, have been crucial to this project. Together we hope that our two young sons, Aaron and Daniel, will have the temperaments and the desire to talk with others (including their parents) about the things that matter most.

Introduction

In the last twenty-five years, the effort to understand the ways of others has reinvigorated religious discussion on many levels. We have entered what one leading Jewish thinker has described as the "Age of Dialogue."[1] But what should be the nature of such dialogue? And what should be its goal? What exactly is the proper relationship between different communities of faith?

In December of 1987, these questions were addressed on the opinion pages of the *New York Times* by Arthur Hertzberg, an officer of the World Jewish Congress, in reply to a statement made by Joseph Cardinal Ratzinger, the chief Vatican theologian. As interpreted by Hertzberg, Cardinal Ratzinger's position is that "a Jew encounters the full truth of his Judaism only by becoming a Catholic."[2] Protesting this assertion, Jewish participants in the formal Catholic-Jewish dialogue that began in 1971 between the two communities canceled their scheduled meetings, arguing that such a position makes dialogue impossible. But Hertzberg argued that Cardinal Ratzinger did nothing offensive; instead, he "cured us of an illusion" and rightly redirected the path of dialogue. According to Hertzberg, Cardinal Ratzinger claimed for Catholicism what most Jews wish to claim for Judaism: "religious primacy." While such a claim does put an end to the development of "a new, liberal theology" which can be professed by both Jews and Catholics, it does not put an end to interreligious dialogue.

> It is thus clear now beyond any doubt that no dialogue that has any theological content can be conducted between the two communities, for such discussions can lead only to increasing anger. But the dialogue is not therefore at an end. . . . The fallout from Cardinal Ratzinger's interview has simply re-established that Jews and Catholics belong to differing religions. The dialogue can now return to its origins, no doubt in a much more sober mood. Jews should continue to discuss with Catholics a whole host of *social and even political problems* in which both communities are involved. . . . Jews and Catholics are comrades in the quest for social justice.[3]

Hertzberg clearly restates the modern approach to the relationship between faiths: people of different traditions who find themselves in close proximity and dependent upon the same resources, and perhaps having a common

1

enemy, must tolerate one another's differences and even cooperate with one another. But they need not, and ought not, go beyond tolerance to a relationship that is not simply "external," concerned with social or political or economic relations, to a relationship that is "internal," concerned with one's deepest convictions about the nature of reality. On the model of the polite visitor who refrains from speaking about religion or politics to his or her hosts, the dialogue between different religions should also shun any critical discussion of the things that matter most: our perceptions of truth.

This book is written from a position that is at odds with the notion that we should engage in dialogue only in order to assure social tranquility and not also as a means for uncovering truth. It should be undertaken for both reasons. Dialogue that joins diverse people together for work on a shared good may lead us into fellowship. Dialogue that extends our understanding of one another, of ourselves, and of truth, may ground that fellowship in deep soil so that its sweet fruit might endure. Indeed, "practical" dialogue — about social problems — and "theological" dialogue — about perceived truths — go hand-in-hand. Theological dialogue is not only possible; it is highly desirable because it is a means for acquiring a fuller understanding and hence a deeper peace.

This book is an attempt to describe a Jewish approach to non-Jewish traditions. Beyond this, it is an attempt to describe a way in which Jews might remain faithful to their relationship with God even as they encounter other traditions. It is based on the assumption that the plurality of faiths is a blessed fact and that the strongest affirmation of this fact — an affirmation of the theological relevance of other religions — is also the more profound way of remaining faithful as Jews to God's presence in our lives.

It begins with an affirmation of *veridical pluralism* and a rejection of both absolutism and relativism.[4] Veridical pluralism is the position that there is a plurality of truth-laden traditions. The truths that are possessed by different traditions, both religious and nonreligious, may be different — that is, they may be illuminative of different aspects of reality, or they may be the same truths expressed differently. Truth itself is coherent — it holds together without contradiction; the partial truths that are known to us through our limited perspectives may thus be different from each other, but not mutually contradictory. There is a universe and it contains a plurality of true expressions. It also contains many incorrect descriptions. Our task, as members of the universe and of particular truth-seeking traditions, is to distinguish between the true and the false and *to make the truth our inheritance, regardless of its progenitors*.

It is in dialogue that we who participate in various traditions which claim knowledge of the truth are challenged to correct, enlarge, restate and/or reform our knowledge. When it is undertaken for the sake of the universe — that is, for the sake of everyone, including ourselves and others, the non-human world and God — it entails the mutual setting forward of our most private and crucial beliefs for the purpose of reaping a fuller understanding of truth. Such dialogue is termed in this essay *transformative dialogue* because serious regard for another's truth claims may well lead to a transformation of one's own self-understanding.[5]

In brief, veridical pluralism assumes both a profound commitment to truth and a wholehearted commitment to a tradition. At the same time, it presupposes the historical conditionality of all traditions and yet stipulates that the hypothesis that they are equally valuable be tested in dialogue. Finally, it requires full openness to the claims of others and the willingness to transform one's own tradition in light of the truth that is found.

Indeed, this book constitutes a methodological prelude to transformative dialogue between Jews and non-Jews or between Judaism and nonreligious outlooks such as Marxism and evolutionary biology. In chapter one, a fuller argument for veridical pluralism is made and transformative dialogue is further explained. Chapter two is a brief overview of the history of the Jewish understanding of non-Jewish traditions. The models that four major modern Jewish thinkers—Leo Baeck, Franz Rosenzweig, Martin Buber, and Mordecai Kaplan—developed for understanding non-Jewish traditions have been formative for contemporary liberal Jewish thought. In chapters three through six, these models are examined in detail, both to illuminate our options and to move us beyond their creators' insights. The final chapter is an imaginative construction of a transformative dialogue, undertaken to show the benefits of such an exchange. While not the result of an actual interchange between a Jew and a Buddhist, it is to be read as an example of some of the possibilities inherent in transformative dialogue.

The point of departure here is the affirmation of veridical pluralism, which requires a new way of approaching other traditions. It is argued that mutually transformative dialogue is the most fruitful way to respond to the fact of veridical pluralism and should therefore be the goal of Jewish participants in dialogue.

1

Veridical Pluralism and
Transformative Dialogue

Because Jews have almost always lived as a minority community whose religio-cultural orientation differed, sometimes more and sometimes less, from that of the majority community, they have been ready advocates of religious tolerance. This advocacy was not a recognition of the truth claims of other religious traditions. Indeed, traditional Judaism seldom (if ever) maintained that other religions were in themselves pathways to salvation. Rather, the Jewish affirmation of religious tolerance was primarily a response to the sociological conditions of the Jewish people. Were Christians and Muslims to establish a policy of religious tolerance, life for the Jewish population within their borders would be a good deal less fragile. Indeed, since religious tolerance is the basis for civic tolerance, the political, social, and economic benefits of religious tolerance would be considerable.

In the late eighteenth and early nineteenth century, there was a significant increase in the level of tolerance that was accorded the Jews who lived in Western Europe. But the basis of Jewish emancipation was not the Christian community's acknowledgment of the truth value of Judaism. What was affirmed was that *despite* Judaism, Jews ought to be accorded some liberties. A position of tolerance was reached on the basis of a general humanitarianism: all human beings, by virtue of their humanity, deserve a certain amount of respect. Important as this insight was, it required no reconstruction of Christianity's understanding of Judaism. Jews, not Judaism, were to be tolerated.

In the main, the emancipated Jewish community did not move beyond this general humanitarian principle. Judaism's own, much older, theory of the natural rights of human beings continued to serve as the framework for assessing the non-Jew. The tradition of the Noachide Laws asserts that salvation is available to non-Jews if they maintain a minimal level of humanity. People of other traditions are to be tolerated—indeed, will be saved—if they adhere to the Noachide Laws. The only "truths" that other religious traditions possess are the "truths" of Judaism, most especially those that are stated in the Noachide Laws.

Neither Christianity nor Judaism proposed that there might be more than one true and salvific tradition. What eventually came to be recognized, however, was the fact that theological absolutism is insupportable. Today we know that the logic of absolutism does not hold. We know it by means of contemporary physics, which asserts that we are limited by our subjectivity and our physical location. We know it through history, with its bloody evidence of the destructive consequences of absolutism. We know it through biblical scholarship, which informs us that our traditional basis for confidence is itself an example of shifting perspectives. And we know it through our personal experiences of loving those who do not share our traditions.

But now we mistakenly believe that we must embrace relativism if we are to avoid the corruptions of absolutism. Relativism, however, has its own serious failings. Most significantly, while it denies any religion the right to assert its truth over that of another, it also results in a negation of the existence of truth itself. Moreover, relativism repeats some of the errors of absolutism; most egregiously, it too makes any real sympathy for another tradition impossible.

Our choices, however, are not limited to absolutism and relativism. We do not need to absolutize our position and hence annul the other's position, and we do not need to abandon the truths we possess in order to make room for other religions. There is a third option, the option of *veridical pluralism*. Veridical pluralism allows us to maintain the insights of modern physics, biblical scholarship, historiography, and existential encounter, insights that remind us of our personal limits and inform us of our fellow beings' capabilities. Unlike relativism, however, it also allows us to hold to the position that truth exists.

Veridical pluralism is the position that there is more than one tradition that "speaks truth" (*verus dicere*). It is based on the principle that reality is one and that truth is coherent. The truths that are spoken by traditions are partial and particular truths, and for that reason they may appear to conflict with one another. But if what a tradition speaks is really true, then it must be congruent with other statements of truth. Veridical pluralism affirms the idea that there may be real and important differences (as well as similarities) between traditions, but that which is true is of necessity compatible with all else that is true. In its affirmation of the partial nature of human understanding, veridical pluralism opposes absolutism and exclusivism. In its affirmation of the oneness and the necessary coherence of truth, veridical pluralism opposes relativism.

Veridical pluralism is not simply the recognition that there are many ways by which humans seek salvation. It is the affirmation that several of these are ways of truth. In other words, veridical pluralism goes beyond the recognition of the fact of plurality to a judgment about the plural forms that fill the world. The human dimension of the world is and always has consisted of a wide variety of salvation-seeking ways, not only religious but also political, philosophical, and aesthetic. Not all of these have generated important truths, and indeed, many have contained serious falsehoods or only trivial insights. Such traditions are clearly inferior to those that embody important truths. In reaching this evaluation, veridical pluralism is distinguished from cultural pluralism, which simply affirms the external fact of plurality but does not attempt to evaluate the internal nature of each form.

Veridical pluralism also differs from inclusivism, the position that there are many traditions that contain truths, but which are true only insofar as they conform to the one, greater tradition. While inclusivism seems to affirm the truth value of other faiths and hence pluralism, it is really a form of absolutism. For the inclusivist, there is only one true religion; all others are regarded as derivative, partial, supplementary, and basically nonessential. By virtue of their relationship with the one mature tradition, they are valuable; to the degree that they stray from the mature tradition, they decrease in value. In contrast, veridical pluralism declares that there may be important truths within another tradition that are not now present within one's own. This recognition is fundamental.

It follows, then, that veridical pluralism moves in a different direction from that pluralism which assumes that the differences between traditions are not essential differences.[1] Although veridical pluralism recognizes that there is a good deal of overlap between some traditions (for example, between Judaism, Christianity, and Islam), it also recognizes that the differences between traditions are no less important — and perhaps are even more important — than their similarities. There may in fact be a universal theology that informs the many traditions, but it also may be that they are really saying different things and not simply the same thing differently. Both the commonalities and the dissimilarities must be relished. The commonalities help us to confirm the truth that we each know separately; the dissimilarities help us to increase and correct our understanding of truth.

Veridical pluralism begins with the premise that *all religious traditions are historically conditioned*. Most modern thinkers assume that religions are historical movements. Judaism and Christianity, for example, have developmental histories and have been shaped by their historical contexts. (They in turn shape those contexts.) In being responsive to their environments, they have changed in important ways. Ideas have been discarded and added, modified and emphasized; likewise, the expression of those ideas has changed. We have, in the last century, especially, greatly enriched our understanding of how religions have been both formed and formative. The realization that religions are historically conditioned has had an enormous impact on our understanding of our own traditions and of the relationship between traditions. Above all it has led us to the ground-breaking insight that that which is historically conditioned cannot be absolute. To claim that Judaism or Christianity or any other religion is the one, complete, final truth by which all individuals shall gain salvation is to commit idolatry. It is to exalt that which is, for all its beauty and power, nonetheless partial, limited, and unfinished.

The impact of the idea of historical consciousness on theology has been as powerful as the impact of the theory of the unconscious was on psychology. And the two insights serve us in similar ways. They both act as limiting devices, as ways of keeping our images of ourselves in check by coming to terms with our histories, in the one case with our external histories and in the other, our internal. In both cases, too, we are forced to recognize how influenced we have been by things beyond us, how much of "our" selves is the consequence of our relations with other selves. And whereas previously our claims for absolutism were limited only by our respect for the unlimited nature of God (and hence, often not very limited), now our claims for absolutism are in direct opposition to our whole understanding of ourselves and of reality.

Thus since historical consciousness compels us to reconstruct our understanding of the relationship between traditions — and has rendered the models of exclusivism and inclusivism obsolete, there are two remaining ways of conceiving of the relationship — the models of relativism and veridical pluralism. Both methods begin with the fundamental proposition that there is more than one legitimate way to truth and salvation. This affirmation has been described as "the crossing of a theological Rubicon," from the conviction of a singular norm to the acceptance of a diversity of valid norms.[2] The two models differ, however, in a very important way not often clarified. Relativism assumes that there is a *parity* between the many traditions; veridical pluralism does not.

Langdon Gilkey articulates the assumption of parity when he speaks about the theological implications of plurality for a Christian theologian:

> That we now speak of theological implications of plurality, and clearly intend *serious* implications, thus bespeaks a new sense or understanding of plurality, a new assessment of its meaning. This new understanding of plurality, therefore, includes and adds the concept of "parity," or of "rough parity," to that of plurality: we recognize, often against our will, that in some sense the sole efficacy or even superiority of Christianity are claims we can no longer make, or can make only with great discomfort. I assume we are all agreed on this, otherwise a serious discussion of diversity and its theological meaning would not be undertaken, nor would serious and authentic dialogue between religions be possible.[3]

The relativist knows of no idolatrous faiths; the other tradition, indeed all other traditions, are equally valid or "roughly" equal *in their own right*.

For the model of veridical pluralism, however, the notion of parity is a *methodological assumption only*. As such, it enables a dialogue in which the participants assume the personal integrity of the other tradition and listen *in hope* for the verification of that integrity. It is analogous to the attitude of objectivity called for by the scientific method. That notion, for all its mistaken assumptions about reality, rightfully attempts to express the same attitude called for by the theological assumption of parity: genuine openness to that which one is trying to understand. The notion of parity is a hypothesis — that there are several equally valid ways. It needs to be tested in dialogue, but the dialogue in which it must be tested would not happen if the assumption of parity were not made. In contrast, within the relativist model, the notion of parity is a foregone conclusion. The relativist judgment of parity prior to dialogue actually renders dialogue superfluous: If all traditions are equally valid, then there is little motivation for listening with anything other than curiosity to adherents of another tradition; there is no moral or existential reason to do so. Moreover, there is no convincing reason to remain committed to one's own tradition. If all paths are equally valuable, the potential traveler is faced with the question, Why choose this path rather than another? A particular path might be more convenient or the one that family members have long taken. But it cannot be claimed that the chosen path is the only true one or the most true one. Vigorous commitment to a tradition is thus difficult, if not impossible, to sustain.

Relativism — the peremptory affirmation of parity between religions prior to investigation — is at best a superficial endorsement of pluralism and tolerance. Other traditions are recognized as valid, but that recognition does not hinge on any in-depth understanding or appreciation for the other. On principle, and not as a consequence of intentional interaction, the relativist affirms the validity of another tradition. In fact, it may be completely unknown to the relativist who nonetheless affirms its validity. This is tolerance at its weakest — tolerance for its own sake, not for the sake of truth. Indeed, it can be treacherous if followed consistently, for it can result in the toleration of evil.

> We knew there were religious cannibals, religious sacrifices of human victims, religious wars of aggression, religious murders, religious castes — and so on. Most of these have been pushed aside in our consciousness through the need, and it is a real need, to be tolerant and to free religion from its baleful faults of intolerance, fanaticism, and unbridled cruelty . . . and twentieth-century experience has also illustrated this point extravagantly. For in our century intolerable forms of religion and the religious have appeared: in virulently nationalistic Shinto, in Nazism, in aspects of Stalinism and Maoism, in Khomeini — and in each of these situations an absolute religion sanctions an oppressive class, race, or national power. These represent the "shadow side" of religion, and they are radically destructive.[4]

In order to act against such evils, we must be able to posit a set of values that is not limited to this or that tradition, but which serves as a transcendent norm by which all faiths are judged and which leads us to the conclusion that not all are equally valid. To postulate such a standard is, of course, to dissolve relativism.

Those people who prescribe relativism as an antidote to the evils of absolutism find themselves in an insufferable position when the antidote no longer stems the poison and may even advance it. When they choose to resist the evil promotions of another tradition, they believe themselves to be without ground to stand on. But the ground *is* there. It is the ground of veridical pluralism.

Veridical pluralism is affirmative both of the modern insight that all activity is culturally conditioned *and* of the traditional insight that there are values that transcend particular cultures. One is not therefore forced into choosing between absolutism and relativism or between particularism and universalism. Like relativism, veridical pluralism upholds the historical and cultural relativity of all traditions. And yet, like the models of exclusivism and inclusivism, veridical pluralism affirms whole-hearted commitment to a tradition. For just as scientists cannot dissolve their subjectivity even as they seek after objectivity, adherents of specific religions need not relinquish their faith commitments in order to achieve an attitude of openness. Openness and commitment are not contrary positions (unless one is committed to a lack of openness). Indeed, commitment is a necessary ingredient for a fruitful dialogue: it is what makes the whole enterprise important and passionate. If one is not committed to a tradition, engagement in a dialogue may be intellectually stimulating or academically interesting, but not crucial. Seen from within the model of veridical pluralism, profound commitment to a tradition and acceptance of its limited nature are not two horns of a dilemma. Only if one does not accept the premise that all traditions have been at least partially formed within the crucible of history, or if one contends that the relationship between all traditions is one of parity, are full commitment to a tradition and full openness to other traditions inimical.

The sort of commitment that one makes to a tradition (or person or institution) in the face of historical consciousness is analogous to an ongoing promise of love. Commitment to one's spouse or one's children is not a consequence of their perfection, and indeed one loves them even as one recognizes their limitations. So too with commitment to a tradition: in spite of that tradition's limitations, and because of what it is and what it could be, we commit ourselves, as lovers, to it.

The denial of the absolute nature of any tradition is at the same time the affirmation of the dynamic character of all religions. Those that span millenia and continents have changed a great deal; in some cases their modern and original forms resemble one another very little. There are, for example, enormous differences between Judaism in the sixth century B.C.E. and in the first century C.E. or between American Reform and Moroccan Orthodox Judaism. The model of veridical pluralism affirms and values the dynamic character of all of these Judaisms. It is a fact that when traditions interact, they often change one another: for example, Judaism affected Hellenism and was in turn Hellenized. Such changes are not necessarily good ones; when made in response to new truths, however, they are very likely beneficial. In order to be faithful to one's own truth-seeking tradition, one must respond to truth no matter who its bearer is. But because of the fundamentally dynamic nature of traditions, the encounter with new truths need not lead to a breakdown of one's own faith or a falling away from it. It *may* have those consequences, but it is not limited to them. The decision to convert after having engaged in dialogue may be a statement about the inability of one's own tradition to incorporate a significant truth adequately. The decision to reaffirm one's tradition without change may be a statement that no significant new truth was encountered. Interreligious dialogue may lead to *conversion* or to a firm *reiteration* of one's faith. But because traditions are mutable, dialogue may also lead to the *transformation* of one's own tradition in response to an encounter with a significant new truth.

Judaism has been most successful in transforming itself (and, in certain important instances, others) in response to its encounter over the centuries with other traditions and cultures. And yet it has been able to maintain a balance between continuity and change. It has been able to integrate many new ideas that were first "alien" but which became "Jewish." And these new ideas were not crudely grafted on so that Judaism became a syncretic jumble. Rather, on the model of a person, Judaism maintained its *personhood*, its self-continuity, even as it grew and traveled, flourished and suffered and aged. This achievement was possible because of the classical Jewish method of self-understanding or self-explanation: commentary. "Commentary allowed different generations of Jews the opportunity to creatively interpret their intellectual heritage within the context of a tradition."[5] Because of this method, the central and defining "story" for Judaism could abide, but a thousand variations on the story could be made.

There are two principal components to the method: *peshat* and *drash*. *Peshat* is the attempt to understand the text as it speaks for itself; the listener approaches the text in a phenomenological way, attempting to hear the unembellished facts that it gives. *Drash* is the existential reading of the text; the reader is free to move beyond the prosaic to a personal and creative interpretation of it. David Hartman discloses the significance of these elements for the method of commentary as a whole:

> Commentary thus involves an interesting balance of potentially contradictory attitudes. *Peshat* demands of the commentator that he subordinate his interests and feelings to the text before him, while *midrash* [*drash*] frees the commentator to uncover personally meaningful insights and attitudes within the given text. The dialectical tension between continuity and change lies at the heart of commen-

tary and explains how Jewish creativity was able to express vastly differing religious orientations without severing its connection to the past.[6]

Jews have long had a way to incorporate new ideas into the tradition without losing its central insights and expressions. And Judaism has a long history of transformative change. The most obvious example is the one that is assumed by the foregoing discussion of commentary — its transformation from a biblical to a talmudic or rabbinic tradition. The decision to write down the oral tradition *and* to give it authority equal to the biblical material was a decision that affirmed both continuity and change. And it was no accident that the written form of the oral tradition included conflicting opinions and arguments; it was a conscious acknowledgment of the dynamic nature of life and hence of religion.

In the preceding pages, veridical pluralism has been promoted as the logical consequence of modern historical consciousness. There is, however, a religious argument, indeed a specifically Jewish one, to be made in behalf of veridical pluralism: the argument based on Jewish theocentrism.

Judaism is a theocentric tradition. What it means to live a Jewish life is to attempt to live in faithfulness to God, to be holy like God, to do God's will, to walk with God, to be responsive to God, to make God the center of one's life so that all of life becomes sanctified. What does it mean to be God-centered in a world in which we are aware of the limitations of our perceptions and truths and religious traditions? What does it mean to be faithful to God's presence in these modern times? Surely it means that we must give up the notion that everything that is important to be known has already been revealed to us. Revelation need not be "contentless," but the content that is revealed cannot be assumed to be fully conclusive. To believe that there is nothing further for Jews to learn about God's presence in the world is to maintain a conceit that limits God and moves toward idolatry of the human mind. What has been revealed may be different from what is being revealed and from what will be revealed. We must work to be fully open to God's message as it is spoken to us now.

Furthermore, in faithfulness to God, we must be truly receptive to the message spoken by adherents of other faiths. To maintain that God speaks only to Jews is corruptive of the nature of God for it imposes a human desire for exclusivity on God, who is not exclusive. And to hold that God speaks best to Jews or to assert, apart from genuine dialogue, that Jews understand best what God says, is an attitude of such presumptuousness that our theocentric focus is blurred. It is precisely the Jewish commitment to God, who is present throughout the world as a loving and communicative parent, that calls for a Jewish affirmation of veridical pluralism. Openness to others is openness to God. In the twentieth century, responsiveness to God takes the form of responding, openly and seriously, to the claims of other faiths. The fundamental theocentricity of Judaism stands as the best reason for a Jewish affirmation of veridical pluralism.

It follows, then, that the only sacred principle in the dialogue process is the principle of full openness in the quest for truth. Such a principle drives us, in this modern world, into the domains of religions other than our own and we are required, *for the sake of our relationship with God*, to come to appropriate terms with them.

Traditionally, the Jewish community has seen itself in relation to the non-Jewish world as the normative religion, compared to which every other religion was inadequate. Yet, non-Jewish traditions were tolerated, providing that they adhered to conditions that Judaism deemed essential. If they satisfied the code of morals, the Noachide Laws, then although they were bereft of value in their own right, Judaism acknowledged their right to exist.[7]

Currently, most liberal Jews approach non-Jewish traditions with an attitude of appreciation. Other faiths are not merely tolerated; they are appreciated for the value that they hold for their adherents. This approach is a genuine advance over the traditional one, for it recognizes that other religions have intrinsic value that is not necessarily derived from Judaism. When we meet non-Jews in dialogue, our task is to learn to appreciate these religions in their own right — apart from any imposition of our value structure on them — and to elicit a positive appreciation of our own tradition from them. We encounter each other as historians of religion, seeking to understand the value that each faith has *for itself*.

Neither of these models is profoundly affirmative of veridical pluralism, of the notion that there is more than one truth-laden tradition. It is with the model of mutual transformation that we are able to recognize not only that other religions may have value for their own adherents, but also that they may have value for those who adhere to other ways. Buddhism, Christianity, Marxism or any other non-Jewish tradition, may also have value *for* Judaism. This is no more than the logical outcome of the recognition that other traditions deserve our appreciation. If they are genuinely valuable and hence elicit our appreciation, then true appreciation must issue in reflexive action, in appreciating the other for myself. Such an encounter with other traditions should thus be understood as potentially transformative of the participants and their faiths. The encounter of religions with one another, when carried on for the purpose of approaching the truth, cannot be restricted to either mutual tolerance or mutual appreciation. For truth, when it is encountered, must not be sequestered: we are naturally and logically led to the process of transformation.

The model of mutual transformation has been given its fullest elaboration by the Christian theologian John B. Cobb, Jr., in his book, *Beyond Dialogue: Toward a Mutual Transformation of Christianity and Buddhism*.[8] Dialogue that begins with the possibility of mutual transformation is very different from dialogue whose intent is limited to mutual appreciation.

> Dialogue with representatives of such groups [non-Christian traditions] would be first and foremost *for our own sake as Christians*. We would hope to enrich our lives and purify our faith by learning from them.[9]

The first purpose of dialogue, then, is self-enlightenment. It is undertaken with the assumption that other religions have something valuable to contribute to our self-understandings, something that cannot be gained, or at least has not yet been gained, apart from such interaction.

Transformative dialogue denies "unintegrated pluralism" and affirms "wholistic pluralism." That is, it assumes that reality is a whole and that true statements about it cannot be contradictory. For example, within this perspective both the Buddhist belief that there is no God and the Jewish belief that there is cannot be true since they contradict one another. But there may be truths reflected in the Buddhist statement that will serve to correct the Jewish statement. The truths of the Buddhist insight and the truths of the Jewish insight will be integrated in such a way that the self-consistent wholeness of reality is preserved. The encounter with other traditions is an undertaking that affirms the wholistic nature of truth, even as it affirms diverse experiences and expressions of truth. Transformative dialogue encourages people to seek after the wholeness which characterizes reality and thus to be enriched.[10]

The wholeness to which transformative dialogue strives must not be confused with vagueness, indefiniteness, or shallowness. On the contrary, when individuals engage in transformative dialogue, they seek to overcome the abstractions and superficialities of their own historical perspectives. They do this by opening themselves up to the insights of others: The result, ideally, is not a loss of insights already achieved, but a deepening of the sense of reality and thus a broadening of the communal understanding.

Nor must the wholeness to which it strives be confused with a denial of particularism. Transformative dialogue is not an invitation to the formation of a universal religion, nor is it motivated by the assumption that all religions are essentially similar. Another way to talk about the exchange it makes possible and encourages has been articulated by the Jewish theologian Eugene Borowitz. What Borowitz calls "the dialectic of Jewish particularity" can also serve as a model for the possibilities and the limits of transformative dialogue.

> My Jewish faith leads me to assert that there is no inherent need to departicularize one's faith because one is drawn to its universal vision of humanity. I suggest that we may find it far more valuable and authentic to acknowledge our simultaneous assertion of particular and universal truths and see how we can envision our particularity so as not to violate our universality.[11]

Borowitz contends that the Jewish affirmation of the universal availability of salvation via the Noachide covenant does not mean either that all traditions are equally worthwhile or that any particular religion is dispensable. Indeed, he argues that universalism requires particularism.

> . . . without a particularistic grounding for universalism I do not see how it can arise. . . . (I)f universality is grounded in particular faith it would seem odd that universality could ever fundamentally negate the truth of particularity for in so doing it would destroy its own legitimation.[12]

Hence, it is crucial to distinguish between "transformation" and "transmutation." Transformation is not an alchemical process in which one entity is changed into an entirely different sort of entity when it is exposed to the right (or wrong) conditions. Transformative dialogue is not a call for participants to depart from their traditions when they encounter something of unique value in another tradition. Indeed, in transformative dialogue a degree of authenticity and distinctiveness is assumed such that the breakdown of a tradition — either through rejection or assimilation — would be understood as a loss for all, adherents and nonadherents alike. Although the immutability of traditions is rejected, transformative dialogue is not a program for haphazard change, simple eclecticism, or reductionism. It is not a call for those who encounter other truth claims to give up their own, to simply add the truth claims of the other to one's collection of such items, or to merge the claims together amiably in such a way that the novelty is lost or trivialized. Something much more strenuous is involved here. What the other person says is spoken to our very beings and the appropriate response is to understand ourselves anew, to reconstitute our self-understanding in response to this new experience. Having met the other, we meet ourselves as newly constituted selves.

It is not always the case that our new selves will be fundamentally different from our preencounter selves. Not every tradition necessarily has something of worth to say to every other, nor are the contributions of different religions of equal importance. Every relationship that takes place in genuine openness should change us, but the degree of change may range from the slight to the significant. That determination of worth, however, cannot be made apart from an actual encounter undertaken in complete openness to the other.

"How can one better serve the universal revealing and saving presence of God than by submitting all that one believes to radical questioning and opening oneself critically to alien ideas?" Cobb asks.[13] Alien ideas made intimate are the means by which our lives and the life of God are enriched, for they strengthen our connectedness with one another. And when these alien ideas are true, mutually transformative dialogue becomes a bid for freedom, replacing "freedom *from* one another" with "freedom *for* one another."[14]

"Freedom for one another" entails not only the opening up of ourselves to the truths of the other, but the sharing of our own truths with our partners in the belief that the depth and power of their religious experiences will also be increased. The purpose of such sharing is neither conversion from one tradition to another nor the confluence of many into one universal religion. Conversion entails a complete turning away from the old; this is not what is demanded by the occasion of truth-sharing. Rather, the encounter with new truths entails a recreating of the old by the new, or again, a reconstituting of the self. Moreover, the goal is not the achievement of a single religious community in which our differences are ignored, degraded or forgotten. The truth should shape us, and when a truth becomes the property of many communities, those communities will share certain similarities and will move, in this way, closer to each other. But the diversity of communities will remain and should be cause for continued serious evaluation and for celebration. Indeed, as Cobb argues, "It is the most radical differences that stimulate the most fundamental reconsideration."[15] The hope is that in presenting the insights of our tradition and in opening ourselves to the insights of others, each might become more adequate to the task of expressing the truths of life.

Dialogue that moves in the direction of mutual transformation sounds different from dialogue whose intent is an airing of ideas. It has a different quality, too, from that which is content with the cultivation of appreciation for diversity. Mutually transformative dialogue is the harvest of these preparatory fields of dialogue. It is commitment to religious pluralism in its most mature form.

2

The Non-Jew Through Jewish Eyes

The traditional basis for the Jewish understanding of and interaction with non-Jewish populations has been the concept of the "Seven Commandments of the Sons of Noah" (*sheva mitsvot bene no'ah*). Applying both to those who lived before the revelation of Torah at Mt. Sinai and to those who lived after but still apart from the Halachic Code, the Noachide Laws provide a framework for understanding both "pre-Judaic" people and "co-Judaic" people.[1] It is a framework that dates back to the period of intellectual construction which followed the destruction of the Second Temple and which is yet operative among many Jewish thinkers today.[2]

Although there have been various lengthier formulations of the doctrine, the standard seven commandments enjoined upon every human being as the basis of morality are as follows: the requirement to refrain from 1) idolatry; 2) murder; 3) blasphemy; 4) incest; 5) theft; 6) the eating of a limb from a living animal; and the positive requirement to 7) establish courts of law.[3] The individual who lives within these parameters lives within a covenantal relationship, the model for which is the relationship between God and Noah. The Noachide covenant is the manifestation of the universal bond between God and humankind. In every case but that of the Jew — who must obey the 613 commandments detailed in the Torah — the individual who abides by the seven Noachide Laws may obtain salvation.

This opportunity for salvation is available in spite of the individual's non-Jewish religious tradition. Indeed, under the framework of the Noachide covenant, the salvific role of non-Jewish religion is rendered superfluous: The blessing of salvation comes through the covenant *alone*.

The degree to which Jews believe that the Noachide covenant satisfies the moral and salvific needs of the non-Jew has varied over the years separating medieval from modern times.[4] Maimonides added the important stipulation that it be understood as a divine revelation, and not as something that could be arrived at through natural means. Those who live according to the Laws of Noah but who do not also recognize the laws' divine origin fall into the category of "sages of the world," and will not be granted a place in the "world to come," whereas those who practice the laws *because* they are divinely revealed are the "righteous of the world" and will be granted a portion in it. For

17

Maimonides, then, it is not sufficient to live an ethical life as outlined by the Noachide Laws; salvation hinges on the recognition that the laws are divine. Moreover, it is clear that, for Maimonides, the Noachide covenant is inferior to the Sinai covenant: what the non-Jew lacks is Torah, and it is only through Torah that the highest relationship—one based on the intellect—is reached between the human individual and God.

The broadest interpretation of the ability of the Noachide covenant to fulfill the religious needs of the non-Jew is given by R. Elijah Benamozegh (d. 1900). In his advice to a man who wished to convert to Judaism, Benamozegh makes clear the power of the covenant of God with the Gentiles:

> . . . In order to adhere to the true religion, in order to become, as you wish to do, our brother, it is in no sense necessary for you to adopt Judaism—that is to say, to subject yourself to the law. . . . We, who are Jews, have ourselves at our disposal the religion intended for the whole human race—the one religion, that is, to which the nations have to subject themselves and through which they may be redeemed and come to stand within God's grace *exactly as did our own Patriarchs before the revelation of the Law at Sinai.* . . . The religion of mankind is *Noachism.* . . . It is that religion that Judaism has preserved, in order to transmit it to the peoples.[5]

In Benamozegh's mind, the relationship between God and the Gentile who upholds the Noachide covenant and between God and the Jew who upholds the Sinai covenant is qualitatively the same.

The more liberal reading nevertheless maintains the root presumption of the more conservative reading: that religious traditions other than Judaism or "Noachism" impart neither moral nor salvific value to the believer. The basis for this contention is the belief that all non-Jewish traditions are essentially idolatrous. It is with reference to this belief that the generations of medieval Jews, with few exceptions, carved out their relationships—both theoretical and practical—with the non-Jewish world.[6]

Rashi, the preeminent tenth-century rabbi of Ashkenazic Jewry, held the classic talmudic position which made no distinction between Christianity and Islam and the varieties of "pagan" religions. All were *ovde avodah zarah*, adherents of "alien worship."[7] A positive appraisal of these non-Jewish religions was inconceivable; the discussion centered on whether members of idolatrous groups *nevertheless* lived within the parameters of the Noachide covenant. This approach is the dominant one within Jewish medieval thought. Even when social and economic factors demanded that Christianity be exempt from the category of paganism, the ideology remained unchanged. Modifications in the practical relations of Jews with Christians were made, but they were argued casuistically rather than by a change in the very principle which gave rise to the problem.[8]

It is with Moses Maimonides in the twelfth century that the equation between the righteous of the world—that is, non-Jews who have a place in the world to come—and the Sons of Noah becomes an uncontested and permanent doctrine in Jewish tradition. As noted above, Maimonides adds the proviso that obedience to the Seven Laws of Noah be in response to the revelatory nature of the covenant. There is yet only one divine religion and that is Judaism. Christianity and Islam are infused with idolatrous elements. Despite their similarities with Judaism, they are to be understood as mere "superficial imitations" of it, akin to a statue shaped in the image of a real man.

> Whereas a person ignorant of divine wisdom or of God's works sees the statue that superficially resembles a man . . . he believes that the structure of the parts of the statue is like the constitution of a man, because he is deficient in understanding concerning the inner organization of both. But the informed person who knows the interior of both is cognizant of the fact that the internal structure of the statue betrays no skillful workmanship at all, whereas the inward parts of man are truly marvelously made, a testimony to the wisdom of the Creator.[9]

If Maimonides' analogy is meant to correspond directly to his understanding of Christianity and Islam, then his criticism of these two major non-Jewish religions is unmitigated. Like the internal structure of the statue, Christianity and Islam betray "no skillful workmanship," and those who mistakenly believe them to be God's works do so because they are totally ignorant of the reality both of their own traditions and of the religion of Judaism. For Maimonides the concept of the Seven Laws of Noah remains the framework within which Jewish-Christian and Jewish-Moslem relations are defined.[10]

It is not until the early fourteenth century that any non-Jewish religious tradition is regarded by a Jewish thinker as having a positive status, independent of Judaism. R. Menachem Ha-Me'iri, representative of a group of Provence rabbis influenced by rationalism, concluded that Christianity, in particular (and Islam, implicitly), could not be classified as an idolatrous faith. Most significantly, he argued this as a general principle and not as temporarily expedient.

Ha-Me'iri's assessment of Christianity is evidenced in his attitude toward Jewish converts to Christianity. Unlike his predecessors, who maintained that it is not possible to shed one's Jewishness and therefore that one cannot abandon the Jewish faith for another,[11] Ha-Me'iri concluded that

> . . . he who has left the fold altogether and becomes a member of another religion is regarded by us as a member of that religion in respect of everything except the marriage laws.[12]

According to Ha-Me'iri, the apostate who "no longer retains the name of Israel" is not "like one who has no religion." Ha-Me'iri recognizes that there are other legitimate fellowships in which an individual may participate. This recognition "has no parallel in the whole of medieval Jewish literature."[13]

This attitude of tolerance, however, has severe limitations: Ha-Me'iri accords value to Christianity not because he determines that it contains unique insights that have been divinely revealed. It is his view that there are moral standards common to all which may be uncovered through reason and apart from either revelation or prophecy. On the premise that Christianity has uncovered these standards and is obedient to them, Ha-Me'iri accepts Christianity as a nonidolatrous faith. Hence, it is the Noachide tradition which yet informs his thought: Christianity and Islam have value insofar as they require of their practitioners a certain level of morality and a means of adjudicating matters which arise in conjunction with these standards. The religions which Gentiles are able to establish, however, are not based on revelation or prophecy, but on ideas that are derived from natural observation, simple reason, the "imaginative power" of political leaders, and/or philosophy.[14] Ha-Me'iri does not consider the possibility that Christianity or Islam may have an understanding of reality that is both true and unique to them, underived from Judaism and yet divine. Hence his positive valuation of non-Jewish religions is minimal.

It is another four centuries before ideas similar to Ha-Me'iri's vis-à-vis other religions are found—this time in the thought of Moses Mendelssohn (1720–1786), the Jew who best embodies the eighteenth-century ideas of religious tolerance. During that period, the Noachide tradition still provided the guidelines for evaluating other traditions. Thus R. Jacob Emden, a leading German rabbi who corresponded with Mendelssohn, could reduce the accomplishments of Jesus to the following:

> The founder of Christianity did the heathen a great good deed by removing idolatry from them, subjecting them to the seven Noachide laws, and thus giving them a *moral doctrine!*[15]

Christianity is to be tolerated because it is not immoral—that is, because it fulfills the Noachide Laws.

With Moses Mendelssohn, the concept of the Noachide covenant is placed solidly within the framework of natural religion. Out of his commitment to the principles of Enlightenment rationalism, Mendelssohn asserts that, "once the degree of a people's enlightenment permits it, all truths that are indispensable to mankind's salvation can be based upon rational insights." That which is necessary and sufficient for the salvation of all people (except the Jewish people, who must continue their obedience to the 613 laws given in revelation) can be naturally obtained and comprehended. Mendelssohn's intellectual bewilderment, then, is genuine when he asks, "Convert a Confucius or a Solon? What for?"[16] One may know the truth, one may live a virtuous life, and one may be saved entirely apart from Judaism.

Every positive religion, according to Mendelssohn, has its "internal" and its "external" aspects. Ideally—and Judaism is the ideal example—the internal aspect of a religion is constituted by nothing more than the principles of natural religion. Judaism, then, has "no doctrines that are contrary to reason . . . the fundamental tenets of our religion rest on the foundation of reason."[17] The external aspects of positive religion give the religion its particular and relative form. These "rules and prescriptions" are distinguished from the essential religious truths which are common to all advanced religions. Thus Mendelssohn reduces Judaism, as well as every other positive religion, to natural religion clothed in a particular pattern. It is not the pattern that is important, but the cloth from which it is cut, and it is clear that the cloth— natural religion—is a revised form of the religion of Noachism, expanded to include all truth arrived at through reason alone.

> According to the principles of my religion, I am not expected to try to convert anyone not born into my faith. . . . Our rabbis hold unanimously that the written as well as the oral laws that constitute our revealed religion are binding only for our own people. . . . All other nations were enjoined by God to observe the law of nature and the religion of the patriarchs. All who live in accordance with this *religion of nature and of reason* are called "the righteous among other nations"; they too are entitled to eternal bliss. Far from being obsessed by any desire to proselytize, our rabbis require us to discourage as forcefully as we can anyone who asks to be converted. We are to ask him to consider the heavy burden he would have to shoulder *needlessly* by making this step. We are to point out that, in his present state, he is obligated to fulfill only the Noachide laws in order to be saved.[18]

The garment worn by Judaism—the commandments revealed at Sinai—is a "needless" mantle for the non-Jew. The "religion of the patriarchs," that is, the Noachide covenant, now broadened to include the "religion of nature," is the means of salvation for all those individuals who have not received a special revelation. Indeed, Mendelssohn states explicitly that special revelation is not necessary in order to attain the ultimate goal of human existence, salvation. "Anyone upon whom God has not imposed these difficult obligations [the 613 commandments] should live according to the law of nature, assured that man, qua man, is innately capable of attaining salvation through righteous living."[19]

Like Ha-Me'iri, Mendelssohn argues for a level of religious tolerance based upon the common truths which may be possessed by all people. And like his predecessor, Mendelssohn recognizes the value of religious traditions which sustain and promote these universal truths. Non-Jewish religions have merit not because they mimic or continue the plan of Judaism. Neither do they have merit because they reveal some unique truth nor because they express a known truth in an exceptional way. Positive religions have value insofar as they reflect the truths of natural religion. Any augmentation of these truths, whether they be legislative, doctrinal, or ritual, has no impact for adherents of other faiths and indeed might either obscure the natural insights which constitute the religion's core or prevent the religion from arriving at those fundamental insights. Such is in fact the case with Christianity as Mendelssohn understands it. Doctrines which are central to Christianity—the Trinity, the Incarnation, the Passion, the Satisfaction, Original Sin—are interpreted by Mendelssohn to be in "outright contradiction of the fundamental principles of reason."[20] The superiority of Judaism over Christianity, and indeed over every other religion, lies in its complete conformity with reason—that is, its perfect actualization of Mendelssohn's revised form of Noachism.

Mendelssohn is the individual by whom the Jewish entrance into modernity is marked. In his public declarations, he confronted the issue which epitomizes religious modernity—the issue of pluralism. Yet his position on non-Jewish religions is in basic harmony with the tradition followed by medieval Jewish thinkers. His inclusion of reason and his concomitant disregard for Maimonides' stipulation that the Noachide code be regarded as divinely revealed is important because it signifies the split between the medieval mind and the modern mind. But the essential measure by which non-Jewish traditions are to be judged remains unchanged: Mendelssohn's affirmation of other religions does not stem from a recognition of their unique achievements or even an appreciation of their novel forms. It is rooted in their adherence to a moral code which is equally accessible to all nations. There is as yet no affirmation of value that is particular to and inherent within a non-Jewish religion.

In the nineteenth century, social and political opportunities for the Jewish population substantially increased. But civic freedom brought with it a new and very difficult challenge: how to reconcile Jewish enthusiasm for the non-Jewish world with continued allegiance to a faith deemed irrelevant by that world. The response to this challenge was twofold. There was the continued reliance upon the Noachide framework as the means by which to affirm the universal and humanistic principles of the day. Indeed, Noachism became "a religion to which most of its members did not know they belonged."[21] In the main, however, the Jewish discussion of non-Jewish religions was vigorously apologetic. In this new environment, Jewish thinkers began a serious study of Christianity. Their conclusions reveal the polemical nature of the Jewish approach to non-Jewish traditions during this period. Samuel Hirsch (1815–1889), for example, explained, or rather explained away, the positive power of Christianity by asserting first that Jesus taught nothing novel but rather, "understood, realized, and fulfilled the idea of Judaism in its deepest truth" and second, that Christianity's mission to the world was no more than the Noachide mission — the preaching of ethics and monotheism.[22] Similarly, Salomon Formstecher (1808–1889) argued that Christianity and Islam "are the northern and southern missions of Judaism to the pagan world; they are the means used by Providence to overthrow the deification of nature and to aid the generations of man to the apex of perfection."[23] These traditions serve the cause of truth only insofar as they bring non-Jews closer to the truth of Judaism, which is, ultimately, the only one true religion. And Abraham Geiger (1810–1874) saw Christianity as the foil to all that was rich and full — to all that Judaism embodied: "Christianity is the true mother of the mystical and the romantic; . . . Judaism is clear, concrete, vigorous, happy with life, and intellectual; it does not deny the mortal world but seeks to illuminate it."[24] This polarity is, as we shall see, later reiterated and expanded by Leo Baeck.

It was Hermann Cohen (1842–1918), the towering German-Jewish thinker of the nineteenth century, who expressed for the first time a sense of some positive interplay between Judaism and Christianity, rather than the one-directional dependence of Christianity on Judaism for its truth.

> Much of what we, as modern men, recognize as alive in our Judaism is Christian illumination which arose out of those old, eternal foundations. Would our current notion of the Messianic idea have been possible without the liberation of the German spirit set in motion by Martin Luther? Or would the development of medieval Jewish philosophy, which was responsible for the intensification of religious life and for its philosophical freedom, be responsible for Mendelssohn? Could Mendelssohn's *Phaedon* or his *Jerusalem* be derived historically or intellectually from Maimonides?[25]

According to Cohen, the influence of Christianity on Judaism had not simply been destructive, as Abraham Geiger, for example, had argued; there was an increasingly productive relationship between the two. Cohen was highly critical of Christianity — he believed that in many ways its rituals and dogmas undercut the major principles of a religion of reason — monotheism and ethics. But his critical assessment of parts of Christianity was tempered by his overall appreciation for it. He was thus unique in arguing at that time for tolerance based on a mutual appreciation, rather than simply as a counter against intolerance: "Neither distrust nor patient waiting should govern our relations with Christians, but tender trust in humanity and human nature, even to our current adversary."[26]

On the whole, however, the Jewish approach to Christianity was apologetic and highly polemical. It was, however, no different from the approach that most Christians took, with less justification, towards Jews. Christian thinkers such as Hegel, Schleiermacher, and Harnack contributed a number of influential interpretations of the relationship between Christianity and other faiths, but in every case, the ultimate superiority of Christianity was affirmed. The understanding of non-Christian traditions was, for the most part, highly superficial. Making a place for those traditions in society did not mean appreciating them for what they were. Likewise, most Jewish evaluations of non-Jewish traditions were also superficial and simplistic. In the encounter of a minority faith with a majority culture and faith, it could hardly be otherwise. Frank Ephraim Talmage summarizes the situation:

> Treatments of Christianity by European Jewish writers in the nineteenth and twentieth centuries have generally followed the pattern set by Christian interpreters of Judaism which may be characterized as a typological approach. According to this, Judaism would be seen as the embodiment of the finest ideas of Western culture, with Christianity viewed as a poor imitation falling somewhat short of the mark.[27]

The Jewish response to religious modernity was doubly defensive since not only was there the task of justifying Judaism to its own adherents, but there was the additional task of justifying Judaism to the Christian world, a world which was in many ways, and especially theologically, still very hostile. Political inclusivism — the fact that Jews were granted citizenship and recognized to be politically equal — did not result in the crumbling of either cultural or religious exclusivism. Describing the relationship of German Christians with Jews in the mid-nineteenth century, Gershom Scholem writes that very few Germans "valued the Jew for what he had to give, rather than for what he had to give up."[28] Despite the political emancipation of the Jews, what they were expected to give up was Judaism.

Hence *the* issue for modern Jews was defined: How or if one could be a Jew and a citizen at the same time. Such dual loyalty had been formally affirmed by the Paris Sanhedrin, but it had been affirmed, in a sense, in the abstract. Once citizenship was an actuality and the ghetto legally dismantled, however, the Jewish community faced the full challenge posed by "emancipation." What exactly had Jews been freed from? And what exactly were they free to do? Had they been freed from their religion and made free to convert? Since the most important social advantages remained closed to Jews despite their "freedom," many Jews did choose to give up Judaism in order to gain entrance into the larger cultural milieu. The task for those who would remain Jewish and yet affirm modernity would now be to define anew the relationship between Jews and Christians, and in the process, to redefine Judaism.

Among the many Jewish thinkers who struggled with the question of interreligious relations in the modern era, there are four whose intellectual leadership was and is formative for liberal Judaism in the current century. Leo Baeck, Franz Rosenzweig, Martin Buber, and Mordecai Kaplan each responded to the challenges that modernity posed, both to the structure of

Jewish self-understanding and to the structure of the Jewish understanding of the non-Jew. Each of these thinkers embraced modernity and each struggled to dispel the idea that modern Judaism was an oxymoron.

Leo Baeck is the most polemical of the four thinkers examined here. His attack on Christianity as "romantic religion" is as much a caricature of that religion as the Christian notion of Judaism as "legalistic." His position vis-à-vis non-Jewish religions is firmly within the boundaries of the traditional Noachide structure, but the frankness with which he expresses his ideas exemplifies the new degree of openness which marked such discussions at the turn of the century. In Baeck's construction, non-Jews are the recipients of the gift of salvation because they stand within the Noachide covenant. The Christian and the Islamic covenants, however, are not considered to be independently salvific; in fact, they may undercut the individual's efforts to live in accordance with the laws of Noah. Baeck affirms cultural pluralism; his is an affirmation of every religion's right to exist, despite the fact that it may be theologically bankrupt. But because he does not affirm the truth value of any non-Jewish religion, interreligious dialogue is limited to establishing and maintaining civic tolerance.

As has often been pointed out, Franz Rosenzweig goes beyond the Noachide tradition in many ways, for he sees the need to speak to other religions with theological respect. His openness is directed exclusively to Christianity, but in this regard he recognizes that Christianity is a revealed religion which has a particular covenantal relationship with God. Rosenzweig's "two-covenant" theory is an advance over those approaches which utilize the Noachide framework as the sole measure of value of all non-Jewish traditions, and he has received high praise for his efforts to attribute an independent worth to Christianity unrelated to either Judaism or Noachism. In this, Rosenzweig moves toward veridical pluralism, and—to the extent that he does so—makes an important breakthrough. It is a breakthrough with serious limitations, however, foremost of which is Rosenzweig's failure to fulfill the intentions of his own method: for in the final analysis, his "two covenants" are one covenant—Judaism—and Christianity is reduced to an auxiliary and temporary construct.

The distance that Martin Buber places between himself and the Noachide tradition exceeds the distance that Rosenzweig is able to travel. First, Buber does not limit his recognition of religious validity to Christianity alone, but extends it to certain non-Western traditions as well, in his assertion that there may very well be more than two covenants. Secondly, he strongly declares Christianity to be a religion whose value is not entirely derived from, subordinate to, or reliant upon Judaism. Pauline Christianity, like Judaism, is an "authentic sanctuary" in which the relationship between God and humanity is nurtured. The I-Thou relationship—*the* measure of value for Buber—can be found within both Judaism and Christianity and, significantly, it is expressed in different ways. Buber's appreciation of Christianity as a unique religion of value does not, however, preclude his vigorous criticism of it, and it is in the harshness of this criticism that Buber comes close to annulling both his positive assessment of Christianity and his affirmation of veridical pluralism. When he argues that the degree of I-Thou immediacy achieved within Christianity is far inferior to the degree achieved in Judaism, the efficacy of Christianity in furthering the I-Thou relationship is deeply impugned. Buber concludes that Christianity is a valuable way for *Christians*, but what it might have to say to Jews remains obscure. Nevertheless, he allows that there is a degree of mutuality between the two religions (and there are some indications that this holds for Buddhism as well) that is not granted by either Baeck or Rosenzweig.

The last thinker to be considered in detail in this study, Mordecai Kaplan, differs from the other three in that he is not primarily an apologist to the Christian community, but an apologist to the Jewish community. His concern is not so much in overcoming the hostility of modern society toward Judaism, but in moderating the Jewish response to American receptivity and restraining the impulse among American Jews to assimilate. According to Kaplan, Judaism is a civilization like any other; as such, it requires no external raison d'etre—it *is* its own justification. Further, Kaplan understands religion as a highly particularistic expression of a civilization that is, essentially, incommunicable to those outside it. This ethnocentrism limits the kind of relationship that can obtain between religious communities to mere physical coexistence. Intellectual or spiritual exchange is not possible. However, there is an opening in Kaplan's thought which makes it possible for him to go beyond the affirmation of cultural pluralism. The novum in modern society is the necessity for "cultural hyphenism," or simultaneously living within two (or more) civilizations. Kaplan's idea of coinclusive civilizations, and by implication of coinclusive religions, is congruent with veridical pluralism.

What each of these seminal modern thinkers proposed in regard to the relationship between traditions shall be the focus of the following four chapters. Although their studies of Christianity were ground-breaking—few scholars had undertaken such an enterprise or had done so with such competence—their work in this area has not been seriously appraised by the Jewish community. Walter Jacob writes that the stature these men have been accorded "was not achieved by their writings about Christianity, which were usually ignored as an eccentricity that had to be tolerated."[29] The time has come to give this portion of their work the attention it deserves. We grapple yet with the questions to which they framed answers; it would be our loss not to stand on their shoulders as we continue the task of living as Jews in the modern world.

Giving serious attention to their work on the relationship between faiths, however, involves being critical of much of what they said and arguing for a position that is different from the ones that they proposed. But the affirmation of veridical pluralism and the call for mutually transformative dialogue — the positions advocated in this book — are shaped by a context quite different from the one in which these men wrote. Baeck, Rosenzweig, Buber, and Kaplan all lived during a time of great political, cultural, and religious turmoil that was to have the most dreadful consequences for the Jewish community. In 1933, the Nuremberg Laws were instituted and once again Jews legally became second-class citizens. But were Jews ever "first-class" citizens in Europe, even when such status was legally mandated? If equality entails mutuality, then most Jews never achieved this position. Between the Jews of Germany and their non-Jewish compatriots, for example, there was little mutuality, without which genuine dialogue is not possible. Indeed, Gershom Scholem writes of the "myth" of German-Jewish dialogue. "To the love of the Jews for Germany there corresponded the emphatic distance with which the Germans encountered them."[30]

The fact that under these conditions, Baeck, Rosenzweig, Buber, and the American, Kaplan, treated Christianity with tremendous respect, recognized the enormous potential and importance of interreligious dialogue, and even attempted their side of such an exchange should fill us with awe and admiration. When even after Theresienstadt, Baeck writes with utmost civility and optimism about the relationship of Jews and Christians, we are given an example of patience, strength, commitment, and openness — a paragon for those of us who enter into dialogue today. In an environment devoid of appreciation or understanding of Judaism, these men undertook to shape a relationship of love. Whatever criticism is offered in regard to their models for interreligious dialogue is a consequence of taking their proposals seriously and not of disregarding either the hostile circumstances in which they wrote or the enormous intellectual debt they are owed.

3

Leo Baeck: Practical Tolerance

In an article written after the Nazi destruction of European Jewry and included in a symposium on post-Holocaust Christian-Jewish relations, Leo Baeck summons Christians and Jews to dialogue:

> . . . now it seems is the season for speaking. On us today it seems, is laid a solemn obligation that the Jewish and Christian faiths meet openly — faiths, indeed, not only boards, writers, or orators. It may turn out one day a sin of omission if they carelessly or timidly or presumptuously shrink from asking and answering the right question. But if they gain mutual comprehension, the task could prove one day even a blessing in the midst of the land.[1]

The questions Baeck poses to the Church are telling not just in regard to the kind of dialogue he envisions, but in his evaluation of religious traditions in general.

> And now, which are these questions that Judaism is in such a spirit allowed, and even obliged, to ask the Church? They will not be designed to challenge dogma or articles of faith: the other's creed is his sanctuary that cannot be queried or disputed here. The subject of our questions is not the "what" but the "how"; that is to say, *not the belief in itself, in its contents, but so to speak the conduct of the belief* — not what the belief wants to say, but how it is saying it.[2]

For Baeck, the content of interreligious dialogue should not be theological. Dialogue should focus not on questions of "dogma or articles of faith," but rather on what Baeck calls matters of "style." "There is a well-known French saying . . . 'the style is the man,' and one could emphatically add: the religion, too."[3]

There are four issues that Baeck marks as the crucial challenges facing a church seeking real dialogue with Judaism. First, he asks if Christians are prepared to relinquish their political power and meet only as religious witnesses to their faith. "[W]hose voice is really heard: the voice of the messenger of the religions or that of an envoy of a regime? — of the faith only, or of an authority?" The Church-as-political-authority has no place in an interreligious dialogue. Second, Baeck raises the same question in regard to missionary activity: Will the Church recognize the right of other religions to proclaim their messages, even to people of other faiths? Will the Church give its assent to the principle that here "there can be no monopolies . . . nor reserved regions"? For dialogue to proceed, the Church must be willing to affirm that Jews (and others) have the right to stake their claims in the world without fear of intimidation and without restrictions on the fulfillment of their missionary tasks. Third, Baeck regards it as essential that the Church understand Judaism *not* as a relic of history, but as a vital and vigorous religion. "Will the Church recognize this full life that is and has been the essence of Judaism?" For it is all too easy to disregard or to defame a tradition that is perceived as fossilized. Finally, Baeck asks whether the Church is prepared to acknowledge its deep rootedness in and strong dependence on Judaism.

> By virtue of the Bible and of the Jewish heritage as a whole, there are in the Church forceful Jewish elements. . . . In a great measure the history of the doctrines that have been striven for within the Church is, one might say, a history of Judaism within the Church.[4]

These last two questions — of the Church's understanding of Judaism and of the Church's self-understanding — may appear to be theological in nature, but for Baeck they are purely historical. That Judaism is an evolving religion of "renascences and revivals" and that Christianity is intimately tied to and profoundly indebted to Judaism are, for Baeck, "plain facts."[5]

Baeck limits dialogue to the establishment and regulation of "noble relations between traditions."[6] He provides rules to make coexistence possible without a compromise of religious integrity. All have the right to witness aggressively to their faiths; none has the right to become an oppressor; there must be the recognition that other traditions have their own inner vitality. These are the guidelines by which the "conduct of belief" of various faith communities — the social and political consequences of religious adherence — is measured and restricted. The intellectual goal of dialogue is "comprehension" (and for the Christian this entails the recognition of indebtedness to Judaism); the practical goal of dialogue, and the goal that intellectual comprehension serves, is the existence "not against one another but side by side."[7] Specifically theological questions about religious beliefs are intentionally bracketed out of the discussion. "The right questions" to be asked and answered in dialogue are the questions that are raised by the possibility of coexistence. How might people of different faiths live peaceably with each other?

Baeck limits dialogue to the "how" of coexistence because he is, for all his universalistic tendencies, a cultural pluralist and not a veridical pluralist. Although he vehemently affirms the right of other traditions to exist and even to missionize, he finally believes that there is only one tradition that embraces truth as it ought to be embraced. That religion is, of course, Judaism. What is known to Judaism can be known to all traditions, but as yet, it is not. God's truth *is* universally available, but the forms and attitudes that religions have imposed on themselves prevent them from properly perceiving or expressing the truth. The essence of all religions should be what the essence of Judaism is: ethical monotheism.

Baeck's Understanding of the Essence of Judaism

In the last public address Baeck gave, he summarized for his German audience the landmark change that separated pre-Emancipation Jewish thought from the thought of Mendelssohn and those who followed.

> . . . now that the world was changed, Judaism had not only to render testimony to itself by its very existence, as had been the case heretofore, but religiously, mentally and, if one may use the word here, theologically also. And this attitude to itself implied an attitude to others.[8]

Jewish existence in the generations before the Enlightenment was its own justification. The need for explanation and for justification both to its adherents and to the outside, non-Jewish community was a demand made by Enlightenment rationalism and universalism. It is the demand to which Mendelssohn responded in the eighteenth century and to which Baeck spoke in the early twentieth century.[9] Religiously, mentally, and theologically, the testimony that Judaism gives in establishment of its self-worth is the testimony for ethical monotheism.

Adolf Harnack's book, *The Essence of Christianity* (1900), was the stimulus for Baeck's own landmark book, *The Essence of Judaism* (1905, revised in 1922). Harnack's efforts to streamline Christianity by lifting it out of its historical context had resulted, Baeck believed, in a serious misrepresentation of Judaism, and thereby, of Christianity as well. Harnack's portrayal of Judaism as legalistic and ritualistic was fundamentally mistaken. In response, Baeck names ethical monotheism as the persistent, defining essence of Judaism.

> No matter when one fixes the date of Israel's birth and no matter what view one may take of its development, one thing is certain: its predominant aspect from the very beginning was its ethical character, the importance it attached to the moral law. Ethics constitute its essence. Monotheism is the result of a realization of the absolute character of the moral law; moral consciousness teaches about God.[10]

In defining the essence of Judaism as ethical monotheism, Baeck places himself firmly within the tradition taught to him by the great neo-Kantian, Hermann Cohen. "The culmination of nineteenth-century thought, of Hermann Cohen's idealistic philosophy and ethical messianism, of the great commandment, the 'Ought,' find full expression here."[11] Although Baeck tempers this neo-Kantian structure with his attention to the Mystery that stands behind and empowers Reason and Commandment, he speaks unhesitatingly of the deed as "proof of conviction."[12] ". . . There is no piety but that which proves itself in the conduct of life and there is no valid conduct of life but that in which religion is realized."[13] In his unwavering emphasis on the practical consequences of religious belief, Baeck is a full-hearted disciple of Hermann Cohen.

Ultimately, Baeck acknowledges, Judaism's life-blood is its theocentricity. "Everything proceeds from the One God, everything returns to the One God. He is the focus of all that is, and all that should be."[14] But Baeck argues that this theocentric nature is best exemplified within the structure of ethical mono-theism. Ethics is understood as the human response to a God-centered reality; it is the way in which humans recognize and express their affirmation of God's qualitative oneness. Ethical monotheism is the "new principle" and the "revo-lutionary principle" which Judaism brought to the world and which created a new world. This revolutionary force ". . . put in its briefest form . . . is the idea and the challenge of the One." And what it means is "that there is only *one* reality — *the one God, His commandment and the doing of it*."[15] Commandment is the language of revelation, spoken by the one God to humanity; ethical action is the language of human assent.

The handmaiden of a theocentric religion is an anthropocentric theology. When, for example, the prophets consider God's attributes, they do so purely for the moral education of humanity: "God is the Lord of the whole universe; therefore we are to love the stranger."[16] This focus on humanity is part of the insight of Judaism that has proved so precious to Western culture. It is rooted in what Baeck calls the "categorical, infinite commandment: 'Ye shall be holy, for I the Lord your God am Holy.' " But for Baeck, only the first part of that command — "Ye shall be holy" — requires exposition; God's existence and God's sanctity are unquestionable. And Baeck's exposition assumes that the primary meaning of holiness is "morality."[17]

In Baeck's Judaism, knowing God and doing right are "synonymous" terms.[18] Faith is understood not as "thou shalt believe," not as a "simple profession of faith in God," but as "the will toward God."[19] The form of revelation is the ethical command, the *Gebot*, and the content of religious experience is not dogma but deed. Here Baeck distinguishes between com-mandment as law, as *Gesetz* (Orthodoxy) or as catechism (Christianity) and commandment as call-to-action. Moreover, Baeck makes a point of distancing his understanding of revelation from the mystical experience of ecstasy and from the romantic experience of "absolute dependency" (although this is not entirely left out). At the same time he rejects a rationalism that would attempt to catalogue the content of revelation. Revelation, according to Baeck, is best understood as an existential event, as the call-to-decision. And faith then is "the choice of one's stand and the way. Its first expression is not in what can be felt nor in what can be conceptualized, but in the decision."[20] The essence of religion is not ecstasy or gnosis which exclude, nor dogma or legal formulation which rigidify and pacify and also exclude. The essence of religion is ethical action, right conduct. Judaism finds its particular expression in, and is the best expression of, ethical action. This religious principle constitutes Judaism's unparalleled contribution to the world and its abiding task in the world.

There is, however, another dimension to Baeck's Judaism besides the ethical. Baeck calls it "mystery," and although it is distinguished from ethics or command, together they form a unity. The mystery is experienced as nonrational consciousness of the Infinite, a consciousness that is felt as an "inner connectedness with God." It is this religious consciousness-of-relationship between the Infinite and the finite that "constitutes the unique ethical basis" of Judaism.[21] The mystery is experienced as "the great unconditional 'thou shalt' " which "arises from the very foundation of reality."[22] The way in which this foundation of reality is presented to the Jew accounts for the enormous influence of Judaism on world history and for the importance of continuing the Jewish presence in the world.

> This problem, through and on account of which Judaism in all its particularity has become universal — this specific problem of world history — is that of the incursion of the Infinite, Eternal, the One and Unconditional into the finite, temporal, manifold and limited, and of the spiritual and moral tension of the moral fiber which is its result.[23]

The "essence" of Judaism is enlarged to include the emotional experience of the "mystery" which yields the ethical struggle. The "experience of mystery" and the "experience of commandment" together form the whole of Jewish religious experience.[24] Baeck joins Hermann Cohen's ethical rationalism with the themes of romanticism, recognizing the "feeling of absolute dependence" and the "experience of the Holy" as legitimate (though insufficient) expressions of the religious experience. Baeck is thus able to forge a "religion of ethical awareness that has remained conscious of its ultimate roots in the Infinite."[25]

Nevertheless, what is described as Baeck's "religion of polarity,"[26] as a dialectic between the poles of mystery and commandment, between nonrational feeling and rational action, is most often described in terms of one pole alone — the ethical pole. The specifically Jewish concern, unlike that of the Christian neo-Orthodox, is not with the moment when divine Infinity enters the finite human arena but with the tensions and tasks that arise therefrom. Moral tension and ethical tasks are the fruits of revelation. Indeed, Baeck defines theology as "systematic reflection" upon these ethical tasks against the background of Jewish history, tradition, and contemporary issues.[27] What we have to reflect upon is *how* people act, for "it is through man's deed that God reveals himself in life."[28] Although there is a mutual interpenetration between the two poles — and that is why Baeck cannot adequately describe the mystery without reference to the ethical, and vice versa — it is the language of ethics that Judaism speaks.

Baeck's Affirmation of Noachism

It is Baeck's fundamental belief that the variety of religious communities with their particular claims about religion have a legal and moral right to exist and to proclaim themselves, even in missionary activities. This right is not linked to any judgment about the truth value of their claims, but only to the fundamental right that every human being possesses as a fact of his or her existence as a human being.

> Our relation to our fellow man is thereby lifted out of the sphere of good will, affection, or even love; it is exalted into the sphere of the established relationship with God, which is common and equal to all and therefore unites all . . . man as such has a claim on us.[29]

The right of all individuals to a dignified existence, regardless of their beliefs, is the divine gift of creation. Part of what one inherits as a child of God is the right to exist as an individual and to be recognized as an individual with such rights by one's neighbors. There is one God who is Creator of all and who has created all in the divine image. This is the ground for the equality of rights and for the unity among human individuals. It is not within the power of the State or of the Church to grant or dissolve these human perogatives. "The conception of right is lifted out of all political and ecclesiastical narrowness and placed upon a purely human basis."[30]

Hence, for Baeck interfaith dialogue presupposes the fundamental right of every community to exist as a religious community and to make the claims which mark it as such. ". . .[T]he other's creed is his sanctuary that cannot be queried or disputed here. . . . Every religion claims its place and asserts its task in the world."[31] Whether or not those claims are true has no bearing on the right of the community to pronounce and propagate them. It is an unconditional given that every individual, Jewish or non-Jewish, and the community with which she or he is aligned, "is entitled not only to toleration, but to recognition."[32] In a culturally pluralistic society, Baeck argues, people have "agreed to disagree" about the absolutist truth claims that are put forward by all traditions. The aim of dialogue, then, is to overcome "practical intolerance" and to humanize "theoretical intolerance."

Where life and living together begin, an upright, living tolerance grows that *does not grant recognition to the other truth*, but understands, with fervent thoughts and feelings, the humanity of other men; thereby it understands, indeed, honors its own steadfastness. *Faithfulness is able to understand faithfulness.*[33]

Tolerance is a consequence of our shared humanity. It is a tolerance of the other's existence as a person and as a religious being; it is not in any way meant to be an assent to the truth-claims of the other's religious tradition.

One ought not to assume that a relationship that arises within such limits as Baeck has set on tolerance need necessarily be lukewarm or superficial. Baeck's childhood experience of the relationship between his father, Rabbi Samuel Bäck, and his family's landlord, a Calvinist minister, informed him otherwise. Their relationship was "warm and intimate" precisely because "each side loved its own tradition and respected the faith of his neighbor."[34] Baeck's position remains the same even after the Holocaust. In the face of the most horrendous evil, Baeck maintained his deep respect for human beings and argued that their right to believe is as basic as their right to exist. Commitment and respect — these are the two polestars of Baeck's theory of human relations. His years in the Nazi concentration camp Terezin only reinforced this conviction.

Baeck understands the Noachide covenant to be reflective of his own model of tolerance. It is, according to Baeck, affirmative of the rights of human beings as human beings based on the universality of God's love. Furthermore, it is not concerned with dogma, but with conduct; no one is excluded from salvation if he or she *acts* piously — that is, abides by the seven Noachide Laws. The acknowledgment of monotheism is the only theological duty placed on the individual; all the rest are the ground rules for maintaining civilization. What the conception of the Noachide entails, according to Baeck, is *not* a recognition of the religious and truth value of the beliefs of non-Jews; instead, it is a "political conception." It is a category which "legally substantiates the independence of moral law and of ethical equality from all rational and denominational limitations." If the non-Jew "performs the most elementary duties of monotheism, humanity and citizenship . . . he has the same legal status as the Jewish citizen."[35]

There is no salvific exclusivism in Judaism, no sentiment akin to that found in the Gospel of John where it is stated that "No man cometh unto the Father, but by me." This assertion was judged by Baeck to be "the harshest and most denominational sentence ever spoken" and the "basis for much mercilessness . . . this sole way of loving God has often left little room for loving man . . ."[36] In Judaism, revelation and salvation, promise and fulfillment, are available to every human being. "Under the covenant, every single human being stands before God. Here, everyone takes his stand beside others. No one stands beneath or above anyone else."[37] Creation, revelation, and redemption are a unity and a possibility for all people, regardless of their beliefs.

For Baeck, then, every individual has the unquestionable right of membership in any religious community, and regardless of what beliefs are espoused, salvation is genuinely available to the pious or ethical within those communities. There is one God, one world, one metaphysical structure — and this is the basis for Baeck's affirmation of universalism and hence of cultural pluralism. There is no special community which has rights exceeding or negating those of any other community. There is no community to whom salvation is not offered by God. In this respect, every human being is equal in the sight of every other human being and in the sight of God. Baeck affirms universal salvation and the right-to-believe of all people, based on their status as creatures of God.

Baeck's Criticism of Dogma and his Evaluation of Non-Jewish Traditions

When Baeck describes Judaism, he uses the language and categories of universalism: the essence of Judaism is ethical monotheism, which is not the consequence of a special revelation but is universally revealed. Yet, when Baeck evaluates non-Jewish traditions, he relies upon the model of Noachism, a model that promotes cultural pluralism, but not veridical pluralism. Noachism assures the individual of salvation, but it does so without any regard for the individual's own tradition. Salvation is not made available because one is a Christian or Hindu or Buddhist, but in spite of one's Christianity or Hinduism or Buddhism. If truth is universal, then why shouldn't Christianity itself be affirmed as a true and saving faith and the Noachide model replaced with one of veridical pluralism?

In answering this question, Baeck secures a place for the particular religion of Judaism in the modern world. His answer hinges on the critical distinction he makes between ethics and dogma.

The efforts of liberal reformers to exchange the ethical structure of Judaism for a creedal one is rejected outright by Baeck.

> No one doubts that Judaism conceives of itself as possessing a revelation and Holy Scriptures; that it proclaims the one unique God and finds in the fulfillment of His commandment the meaning of being human; that it demands the imageless worship of God; that it preaches the purity of the soul and atonement and promises a life in eternity; that it places his fellow man before man; that it teaches the election of Israel; and that it indicates as its realization also the messianic goal, the future. No one doubts that all this is peculiar to Judaism and to no other religion in the same manner. *The objection is raised only against the claim that Judaism possesses dogmas, and the objection is based simply on the exact meaning of the term.*

This meaning shows that Judaism possesses no dogmas, if for no other reason than that it lacks the authoritative institution which would have been empowered to proclaim creedal statements as dogmas and to enforce them as such.[38]

Baeck's repudiation of the idea that Judaism possesses dogmas appears to be based on a strict definition of the word. According to this definition, dogma consists of three characteristics: it refers to a revelation; it has a precise, conceptualized form; and it can be determined, imposed, and regulated by an authoritative power. Judaism never had the structure of authority necessary for its enforcement; thus, by definition, Judaism is a nondogmatic tradition.[39]

But there is a more subtle and much more important argument being made here than the argument-by-definition. It has been said (and what follows is support for this) that Baeck's lifelong intellectual preoccupation was to defend Judaism against the pejorative picture drawn by liberal Christianity and to do so by engaging in a persistent polemic against Christianity.[40] When Baeck denies that dogma is a part of the Jewish tradition, he does so not merely because its criteria are not fulfilled, but because he defines dogma as the opposite of ethics. Baeck notes that ancient Christianity itself distinguished between dogma — statements of faith — and ethical principles. He then uses the Pauline caricature of Judaism as legalism (which Harnack perpetuated) against that which is peculiarly Christian — dogma. Dogma is equated with the negative attributes of legalism: it promotes shallowness, externality, fixity, exclusiveness, passivity, and finality. The hypostatizing of dogma is "something specifically Christian and ecclesiastical, and not only historically, but also in accordance with its essential character."[41]

Baeck argues that the dependence on dogma is a consequence of the notion that salvation is mediated through the sacraments. "An ecclesiastical sacrament cannot be depicted without a dogma. This salvation demands knowledge of salvation. . . . Therefore the believer has to be presented with the final irrefutable knowledge, namely the dogma. Like the sacrament, the dogma also must be received."[42] What is received is a confession of faith *in the church or denomination.*

> . . . the *church* believes, and individuals believe this belief of the church . . . they believe because it is the belief of the church. Because the church in this manner defines the belief of all who are a part of it, it must fix the dogma, this authoritative, irrefutable expression of the belief of all. . . . There is no true church without dogmas.[43]

In contrast to a Christianity that is characterized by its dependence on dogma, Baeck offers a Judaism that is characterized by its focus on ethics. Ethics requires characteristics that are anathema to dogma.

Judaism has never formed a church; it has, according to its essence, fashioned the community. The conceptual starting point in the church is the believing church; in the community, it is the faith of the individual. Every individual, by right and obligation, is the bearer of belief; therefore the individual, not the church, is the bearer of tradition, and that tradition, in turn, is not mere transmission of tenets but also includes the demand to inquire. Possession is preceded by searching. This commandment to inquire is the opposite of dogma.[44]

Unlike dogmatic religion, ethical religion encourages individuality, personal decision and responsibility, and free inquiry. "Free will, responsibility, and conscience" were uttered by the prophets in the same breath as God's existence and sanctity.[45] Moreover, a religion that is centered on ethical action lifts up its unfinished nature as that quality which guarantees its vigor. Part of what is required by the ethical life is the participation of each individual in the struggle to interpret anew that which is received and to contribute to that which is passed on. The "commanding faith" is communication between God and the individual *within* history; revelation is ongoing. Baeck contrasts the prophetic Word — "a living and personal confession of faith which cannot be circumscribed by rigid boundaries"[46] — with the sacramental or dogmatic Word, which glories in its absoluteness and finality. In its claim for finality, the sacramental Word, like the system which it crowns, inevitably breeds self-righteousness and self-satisfaction, which almost as inevitably lead to intolerance. And what it is *most* intolerant of is the "living development of truth."[47] In contrast, Baeck argues that it is fundamental to Judaism, and borne out by Jewish history, that "the traditionally received doctrine was not accepted as something final but rather as a force constantly renewing itself in the consciousness of the community."[48] Ethical renewal is at the heart of the "commanding faith." And while the demands placed upon individuals in this community are great, they are not so heavy as those that are tied to the dogmatic yoke of a "commanded" faith.[49]

Baeck's criticism of dogma, then, is twofold. Dogmas delineate the posture of faith as propositional; "believing that" is given greater import over "believing in." The emphasis on content, Baeck believes, results in a corresponding deemphasis on deed, on the doing that is inspired by "faith in." Furthermore, the nature of dogma is rigid, authoritarian, and absolute. These qualities work against a life of free inquiry, personal decision, and contextual action. Baeck objects to both the content of dogma — theological propositions — and to its form — static affirmations. In contrast to ethics, dogma has only a tenuous connection to religion as Baeck understands it.

When Baeck describes Buddhism as a world-negating faith that is private and pessimistic, and when he describes Christianity as "romantic" religion and characterizes it as subjective and passive, he places these traditions on the opposite side from ethics. It thus becomes clear that he believes that there is only one religion that is ethically oriented and thus truly valuable. That religion is Judaism.

According to Baeck, Judaism and Buddhism are the two "fundamental and determining forms of religion."[50] They are, however, polar opposites and Baeck broadly describes their opposing features as follows:

> The former [Judaism] declares the world to be the field of life's tasks and offers a moral affirmation of the value of man's relationship to the world by deed and will; the latter [Buddhism] declares that man's task is to devote himself to self-meditation without the exercise of his volition. The one is the expression of the command to work and create, the other of the need to rest. Judaism leads to the desire to work for the kingdom of God in which all men may unite, while Buddhism leads to the desire to sink into the One, into nothingness, there to find deliverance and salvation for the ego. Judaism calls for ascent, development, the long march toward the future, while Buddhism preaches return, cessation, futureless existence in silence. Judaism seeks to reconcile the world with God while Buddhism tries to escape from the world. Judaism demands creation, new men and a new world; Buddhism seeks "extinction," departure from humanity and from the world. Thus Judaism is a religion of altruism, since it declares *that* man to be striving toward perfection who has found his way to God by seeking his brethren and who serves God by loving and being just to them. Buddhism, on the other hand, is the religion of egotism, since it attributes perfection to the man who retreats from mankind in order to discover the only true approach to himself.[51]

While Buddhism is a world-negating tradition, working for release from responsibility and involvement, Judaism is a world-affirming religion; its optimism takes the form of ethical action within the community.

Religion, by Baeck's definition, must be "in" the world; the Buddhism of Baeck's understanding — clearly a superficial understanding — is in this sense not religion at all. The polarity, then, is not between two final forms of religion but between that which *is* religion — the classical form that is Judaism — and that which is not.[52]

> Whoever feels the need for religion, whoever seeks in religion a definitely religious relation with the real world, must regard the religion of Israel as a revelation. This means that Judaism is the classical manifestation of religion.[53]

Baeck's description of Christianity is not unlike his Christian contemporaries' description of Judaism. It tends toward caricature, being largely inattentive to the subtleties and tensions within an historical tradition and mostly concerned to identify a structure that is monolithic and consistent in thought and practice. The monolith that Baeck calls Christianity is a composite of two disparate traditions — that which is Jewish or "classical" religion, and that which is Hellenized, or "romantic" religion. Christianity is not a higher creative synthesis of these two traditions; it is not really a tradition unto itself. Paul, its founder, exemplifies the romantic character and the character of the romantic religion: He is "not so much a creator of ideas as a connector of ideas." Judaism is corrupted in this linkage, but the pagan mystery religions are empowered and advanced. Paul's skill lay in knowing "how to fuse the magic of the universal mysteries with the tradition of revelation of the secrecy-wrapt Jewish wisdom. Thus he gave the ancient romanticism a new and superior power — a power taken from Judaism."[54] The central theme of Baeck's argument is evident here: that which is worthy in Christianity has the mark of Judaism on it; that which remains, the romantic elements of Christianity, are agents of weakness and even depravity, and they are antithetical to Judaism.

Baeck borrows the distinction made by Christian scholars between the Christianity of Jesus and the Christianity of Paul. But Baeck claims Jesus and the Gospels for Judaism. It is Pauline religion that is romantic and sharply opposed to ethical monotheism. Paul is the importer of romanticism: in his enchantment with it, he breaks with Judaism. Jesus, in contrast, is "a man who is Jewish in every feature and trait of his character, *manifesting in every particular what is pure and good in Judaism.*" He is "a Jew among Jews" and the Gospels are "a Jewish book in the midst of Jewish books."

> It is a Jewish book . . . because a Jewish spirit, *and none other*, lives in it: because Jewish faith and Jewish hope, Jewish suffering and Jewish distress, Jewish knowledge and Jewish expectations, *and these alone*, resound through it.[55]

The difference between Paul's romantic religion and Judaism (and Jesus' faith) are sharply delineated:

> One might characterize the Pauline religion in sharp juxtaposition: absolute dependence as opposed to the commandment, the task, of achieving freedom; leaning as opposed to self-affirmation and self-development; quietism as opposed to dynamism. There the human being is the subject; here, in romantic religion, the object. The freedom of which it likes so much to speak is merely a freedom received as a gift, the granting of salvation as a fact, not a goal to be fought for. It is the faith that does not go beyond itself, that is not the task of life; only a "thou hast" and not a "thou shalt." In classical religion, man is to become free through the commandment; in romantic religion he has become free through grace.[56]

The difference between the two traditions follows the dichotomy between ethics and dogma. Insofar as Christianity emphasizes dogma, it fails as a religion.

The Jewish elements of Christianity reappear throughout the centuries, especially whenever Christian thinkers attempt to reestablish the primacy of ethics within the church. When Pelagius urges that good works can bring salvation, his argument is "a Judaic one." Socinianism and Anabaptism are movements within Christianity which indicate "a fertile Jewish influence on the life of the Church." Indeed, for Baeck, whenever faith is considered "moral faith . . . in the end this means Jewish faith."[57] Thus Baeck is able to interpret many of the forms of modern Protestantism as pointing "out a way that leads from the early church in the direction of the spiritual and religious realm of Judaism." To be sure, Baeck notes, there has been fierce opposition to the Judaic presence within Christian thought. But the success of these non-Jewish legions, notably those of Augustine and Luther, leaves a plundered Christianity. "The history of the church has shown what there remains of Christianity when it has been purged of everything Jewish." What is left when the church is stripped of its "active, strongly ethical-psychological individual Judaic element," is the "passive, magico-sacramental faith of Paulinism."[58] In these latter attributes, Baeck can see nothing of value.

For Baeck, Christianity finally has no status as an independent religious tradition. It is Judaism plus Greek mystery cults, held together by an authoritative power structure. The truth that it contains is partial and representative of the Judaism that composes its core. To the degree that Christianity conforms to the standards set by Judaism — to an ethical orientation — it possesses religious value. To the degree that it wavers from Judaism, it wavers from the truth.

In summary form, Baeck's argument is as follows: The essence of Judaism is ethical monotheism, which is the only proper content of religion. Since Judaism is the *only* religion that is centered on ethics, Judaism is the only veridical faith. The difference between Judaism and non-Jewish traditions is not a difference in form, but in kind — a system of ethics as compared to a system of dogmas.

Judaism's Mission

The source of Judaism's unique status is the covenant that was made between God and the people of Israel at Mt. Sinai. Baeck revises the notion of chosenness so that it is not in contradiction with the universality of ethics, the impartiality of God, or the equality of all people. While his reinterpretation denies the traditional Jewish belief that the God-of-all chose one people to be the Chosen People, Baeck yet advances a special and ultimate role for Jews in the world.

In Baeck's understanding, God did not "choose" the Jews but presented them with an offer or "command" identical to that which God made (and continues to make) to all people. "Covenant," the classic term for this offer, describes the "great interrelatedness, the great unity of all" and is in fact the "prerequisite for reality itself."[59] Covenant is the religious expression of the metaphysical reality that all life is interrelated because all life is dependent upon the One God. "Nature and morality thus share *one* origin, *one* root; they emerge out of the One. Together they are the covenant, the law of the One God."[60] This universal covenant which is the foundation of all existence is the covenant of God with Noah and his children.

> And as for Me, behold, I establish My covenant with you, and with your seed after you; and with every living creature that is with you, the fowl, the cattle, and every beast of the earth with you . . .[61]

It is because of this covenant that every human being has the potential for participating in creation, revelation, and salvation.

The Noachide covenant precludes the establishment of Jewish chosenness on metaphysical grounds. There is no generic difference between the Jewish people and others. Baeck proposes instead that the grounds for Jewish particularity are *psychological* and *historical*: At a certain point in history, a turning point for world history, the experience of being related to God was felt so intensely by the people of this community that they chose to dedicate themselves to doing God's will. The historic moment in which they recognized the divine commanding presence in their midst was the moment of religious consciousness; the moment in which they made the decision to consecrate themselves to God was the moment of religious self-consciousness. "The knowledge of God and the knowledge of self became a unity that remains indivisible in this people."[62] The people of Israel came to identify themselves as God's people, as self-conscious participants in the covenant. Thus was a particular covenant cast between this people and God:

> Now therefore, if ye will hearken unto My voice indeed, and keep My covenant, then ye shall be Mine own treasure *from among all peoples*; for all the earth is Mine; and ye shall be unto Me a kingdom of priests and a holy nation.[63]

This covenant with Israel does not abrogate or succeed the covenant with Noah; indeed the content is unchanged. It is, rather, an exemplification of the universal covenant. The Jews have become the first people to live self-consciously within the covenant relationship. They have actualized that which is given in revelation as a possibility to all people.[64] "Throughout the covenant, the laws, the world exists." Here Baeck refers to the universal covenant, which establishes the existence and interrelatedness of all reality and its dependence on the one God. "But within the world of man it [the covenant] exists first and only through him; *he creates its existence*."[65] At Sinai the Jews "hearkened unto" the universal message—they chose themselves—and it became embodied in them and they became an embodiment of it. "Therefore as long as this people remains true to itself, there is no place within it to differentiate, let alone to contrast, its consciousness as a people and its religious consciousness."[66] The universal concept was embodied in a particular people and the particular people took on a universal task. That task is to teach people how to choose God and thus be chosen. The belief that Jews are the chosen people of God, reinterpreted as it is by Baeck, does not violate the universal nature of God or of ethics.

Jewish particularism is for the sake of universal truth. The truth that is given in God's ongoing revelation to the world is the truth of ethical monotheism, and because that is the essence of Judaism, the Jewish people serve as *the* example of how the divine-human relationship ought to be actualized. Hence, the Mosaic covenant becomes inseparable from the Noachide covenant.

Indeed, Baeck goes as far as to contend that since the Sinai event, the Noachide covenant ultimately depends upon the Mosaic covenant. In the Noachide covenant, God has reached out to humanity; in the Mosaic covenant, humanity as represented by Judaism has reached back. In reaching back, Judaism has become endowed with the messianic spirit and Baeck applies the name "Messiah" to the nation of Israel, the servant of God.

> This picture of the Messiah passes into that of his people, the people of Israel, whose path is the path to this future, and whose history therefore becomes Messianic history, the history of the future. The destiny of humanity is Israel's destiny, and Israel's destiny is that of humanity. The obligation that has been laid upon it is also the promise that has been given to it. Therefore the people of this religion comes to be the Messiah. "I the Lord have called thee in righteousness, and have taken ahold of thy hand, and kept thee, and set thee for a covenant of the people, for a light of the nations; to open the blind eyes, to bring out the prisoners from the dungeon, and them that sit in darkness out of the prison house."[67]

Israel is not merely the messenger of God's revelation. The people of Israel is "to serve to reveal to humanity God's covenant with it, what God's law and his mystery have expressed. *Through this people, too, humanity shall come to experience God.*"[68] The direct revelation of God to Israel has now become the revelation of God *through* Israel. Baeck has secured a place for Judaism that will not become irrelevant with time.

Baeck does not believe that his claim for Judaism's universalism is also a claim for Judaism's absoluteness. In fact he believes that Judaism is unique in its ability to avoid the extremes of absolutism and relativism which characterized Protestant thought of his day. Baeck offers a distinctively Jewish alternative when he describes relativism or "historicism" as the movement that resulted in revelation becoming "a predicate of history." This "crisis of historicism" was combatted by the absolutists who retained "both the determined situation and the determining norm . . . history became a predicate of revelation." One specific moment, the moment of God's revelation, was established as that which is normative *once and for all*. Baeck argues that universalism can be achieved without the absolutizing of an historical moment. History and theology need not be separate nor must one be subordinate to the other for according to Baeck, universalism "is realized when an idea emerges from a single or collective individuality as a *living spiritual force* which can no longer be physically or intellectually removed from the collective life and thought of humanity."[69] The idea that defines Judaism — the incursion of the Infinite into the realm of finitude and the moral tension that results — "stands opposed to that universal idea of the finished and perfected."[70] The specific problem that Judaism articulates for humanity is this: finite creatures can never complete the task which is theirs by the grace of God. Perfection and the complacency it engenders are revelation-denying postures. An idea that is universal must be expressed within the ongoing events of history, else it loses its quality of universalism. The idea itself has a permanent essence, but the essence is characterized by the power of self-renewal. Ethical monotheism is both the permanent essence of Judaism and the source of Judaism's continual growth and self-modification. "The old revelation ever becomes a new revelation and Judaism experiences a continual renaissance."[71] In Baeck's alternative to absolutism and relativism, revelation is not "dogmatized" — "it has its manifoldness and its movement . . . so that it [is] constantly revitalized, reshaped and born anew."[72]

The dynamic nature of Judaism enables it to be responsive to God's continuing revelatory presence. Its dynamism, however, is characterized by Baeck as self-renewal, as a process of reaching into oneself, and not in any sense as self-transcendence, as a process of reaching out for the novel. The effort to look beyond Judaism for truth is futile because no other tradition has appropriated God's revelation of ethical monotheism to the extent that Judaism has. Baeck refers to the Jewish people's "genius for religion,"[73] meaning the religious self-consciousness that originated at Mt. Sinai. Because of this religious genius, the covenant between God and Israel is an everlasting covenant; accepted by one generation, it cannot be dissolved by future generations. "It shall not depart out of thy mouth, nor out of the mouth of thy seed, nor out of the mouth of thy seed's seed."[74] It is to be renewed by the generations, each in its own way, but the process of renewal is contained within the parameters of Judaism itself.

> This inward power, this capacity to produce and shape and grow, is peculiar to the religion of Israel. . . . At an early stage it became conscious of it, and this consciousness found expression in the assurance that Israel was an elect nation and in the *conviction that the goal of all history was contained in the election.*[75]

Judaism's development is inward; it is a matter of internal renewal. But the development of all other traditions, Baeck argues, is outward, toward the truth that is Judaism. Judaism is the goal because it is the purest exemplification of the divine-human relationship. And for Baeck, the fact that there is only one order of reality means that there is only one path to understanding that reality. "The *One* God can only mean *one religion* to which all men are called and which can only find its complete historical fulfillment when all possess it."[76]

Judaism is not a *completed* religion because it is still working for universal acceptance. Yet it is *the complete religion*, the religion which lights the way to God's truth. The special religious consciousness that is the possession of its adherents needs no external emendations.

Baeck ends *The Essence of Judaism* with a concise statement of his position on the relationship between Judaism and other faiths.

> We acknowledge the treasures possessed by other religions, especially by those that sprung from our midst. He who holds convictions will respect the convictions of others. Filled with reverence for its tasks, we Jews realize what our religion really means. We know that there can be applied to it the words of one of the old Jewish sages: "The beginning bears witness to the end, and the end will at long last bear witness to the beginning."[77]

Other traditions are respected, especially insofar as they reflect the insights of Judaism. These traditions should be tolerated, but Judaism alone deserves serious regard. In the end, all will recognize this to be the truth.

Critical Reassessment

It is Baeck's deep regard for the individual and the rights that belong to the individual by virtue of his or her membership in humanity that is most characteristic of his thought. Baeck's appreciation for all people is rooted in his understanding of God as the one Creator of all. The relationship between every individual and the Creator is the reason for the unity and the equality of all people. Moreover, it is creation that guarantees salvation.

Baeck uses the language of covenant to express the fact of the relatedness of all life to God and hence of the interrelatedness of all life. Traditionally understood as a metaphysical reality, the notion of chosenness is reconceived by Baeck to be descriptive of a psychological and historical event only. God did not favor the Jews over all others; the Jewish people are not the chosen people but the "choosing" people, choosing consciously on one momentous occasion to identify themselves as a people-related-to-God. The covenant made on Mount Sinai is not metaphysically different from the covenant made on Mount Ararat — that is, from the Noachide covenant which describes the relationship of the non-Jew with God. Baeck affirms both an equality of human rights and an equality of divine dispensation based on the common humanity of all.

As a result of our common humanity, there is a natural sympathy and respect for the other and for the community in which the other resides. There is an intuitive level of mutual understanding between individuals such that "faithfulness is able to understand faithfulness."[78] Both on the intuitive level and on the intellectual level, the right of all individuals to witness aggressively to their faiths and the right of no individual to oppress another are affirmed. On this level, Baeck's regard for the personal integrity of every individual is extremely valuable.

But in emphasizing individuality, Baeck tends to deemphasize community, especially the communal aspects of life which are formative for the non-Jew. A major difference between the Noachide covenant and the Sinaitic covenant—a difference which Baeck does not directly acknowledge—is that the Noachide covenant is an account of the relationship between the individual and God while the Sinaitic covenant is an account of the relationship between a community of individuals and God.[79] Within the Noachide framework, value is accorded to the individual but not to the individual-in-community. Hence Baeck, in relying on the Noachide framework, deprives the non-Jew of what he considers to be essential to Jews and a cause for celebration: peoplehood. Indeed, by not recognizing the social nature of non-Jews, Baeck comes close to creating a metaphysical split between Jews and non-Jews and hence undercutting his position on the equality of all. Baeck's failure to address the communal dimension of non-Jewish life is indicative of his lack of appreciation for the diverse ways in which the human population lives out its days. Baeck's desire for the peaceful coexistence of members of different faiths—the motivating ideal behind his efforts at interfaith dialogue—cannot be aided by abstracting the individual out of his or her community. For dialogue to be productive, it must be recognized that individuals live within historical, cultural, and religious communities and are shaped by these communities. Dialogue must take place between individuals *as participants in diverse communities*. Then the individuality of persons can be taken seriously and the pluralistic nature of human life affirmed.

Baeck's attention to the "conduct of belief," to the social and political consequences of religions, is an important corrective to the psychological approach to faith which was popular at the time he wrote. However, in equating religion with ethics, he sacrifices much of its richness and much of what there is to appreciate about and to learn from other faiths. There are three major ways in which he limits the exchange between religions in this regard.

First, Baeck maintains that what people have to share with one another are codes of behavior and not visions of reality, ways of acting and not ways of thinking. Not only does this not seem to be the case empirically—for example, the Buddhist and the Jewish understandings of reality sound markedly different—but it also seems contrary to our intuition about the nature of the relationship between thought and action.

Second, the reduction of religion to ethics requires that Baeck systematically deny the plural forms that Judaism as well as other world religions have taken. Judaism, for example, is purged of both its mystical elements and the "dogmatic" articles of philosophical rationalism. The artificiality of this approach is most striking in his picture of what remains of Christianity after its dogmatic bark has been stripped away. The religion of Christianity, thus reduced to Christian ethics, is judged by Baeck to be derivative of Judaism and inferior to it. Any exchange that might take place would be one-directional, from Judaism to Christianity.

Third, Baeck rules out the possibility that there is something of value to be gained from communities that are not self-consciously dedicated to the ethical life. Might not the ethical life be enhanced by aesthetic and intellectual insights? Any attempt to define the essence of religion will result in a weakening of the ability to appreciate the diversity of religious experience and the manifold ways in which it is expressed.

Finally, Baeck's effort to avoid the snares of relativism and absolutism is particularly relevant to a discussion of pluralism. He contends that what is fundamental to Judaism — the commandment to be holy — "stands opposed to that universal idea of the finished and perfected." Baeck argues that there is no final form of Judaism, and his beliefs that revelation is an ongoing process and that Judaism has no dogmas are supportive of this contention. Because Judaism is constantly reshaping itself in response to the unfolding revelatory truth in history, the life of Judaism cannot be captured in one absolute moment. For Baeck, then, change is an essential part of Judaism's present strength and future vitality.

A Judaism that embraces change and makes no claims of absolutism is ripe for the kind of transformative dialogue which a strong commitment to religious pluralism can yield. It is most unfortunate, then, that Baeck obstructs his path to it by limiting change within Judaism to an internal process, to "self-renewal" and "renaissance." Judaism is powered by its own inward life; its interest in other religions could not be for the purpose of self-enlightenment. Though it awaits completion, Judaism is yet a *complete* religion.

In his neglect of the role of community for the non-Jew, in his reduction of religion to ethics, and in his picture of Judaism as self-sufficient, Baeck limits the relationship of Judaism with that of other religions to that of tolerance. But in his emphasis on the relationship of every individual with God, in his attention to the social and political consequences of religion, and in his rejection of an absolute form of Judaism, Baeck points the way toward transformative dialogue within a pluralistic context.

4

Franz Rosenzweig:
Complementarity Without Parity

Dialogue, for Franz Rosenzweig, is not one among several ways to communicate, nor is it restricted to the exchanges that take place casually and routinely. It is the mode of communication for *all thought*, indeed it is the only proper way *to think*. It is dialogue or "speech thinking" that Rosenzweig prescribes as the cure to the ailing philosophy and theology of nineteenth-century Germany and it is dialogue in the form of a sustained conversation that, in the original sense of the word "converse," turned Rosenzweig's own religious life around.

In asserting that dialogue is the essential method for uncovering and establishing truth, Rosenzweig affirms certain conditions that make for genuine interchange between individuals: the belief that the relationship between real individuals is the arena in which truth unfolds; the recognition that human knowledge of truth is incomplete and hence an attitude of openness to the sources from which further truth may come; the position that time is irreversible and that the future can be anticipated but not known; and the affirmation that freedom, mutuality, spontaneity, and subjectivity are prerequisites for dialogue and hence for real thought. Moreover, Rosenzweig maintains that the content of dialogue must be theological and philosophical in nature. Dialogue is undertaken for the purpose of defining and defending one's orientation in the world by answering the "so-called 'ultimate questions' concerning God, man and the world."[1] Unlike the Reform Jews of his day, represented in this study by Leo Baeck, Rosenzweig does not limit either the purposes or the parameters of dialogue. While Baeck calls upon religious communities to promulgate civic tolerance alone, Rosenzweig asks, "How else can religions be tolerant or intolerant except in theological terms?"[2] Dialogue is fundamentally a conversation about theology and philosophy (which are, according to Rosenzweig, inseparable), not a means of fixing a standard of public conduct.[3]

Rosenzweig is the shaper of a new kind of interfaith discussion largely because of his emphasis on dialogue as the indispensable tool of the truth-seeker and his contention that interfaith discussion must take place on a theological level. His correspondence with Eugen Rosenstock-Huessy, a Christian, has been called, "the most perfect example of a human approach to the Jewish-Christian problem."[4] Over a period of four years, the relativist Rosenzweig was challenged to come to a nonrelativistic position, and then challenged to defend the position, Judaism, which he chose. This dialogue was first an impetus for and then an intellectual expression of the religious experience which brought him back from what he had thought to be inevitable — his own conversion to Christianity — to complete immersion in Judaism. Yet it is indicative of the kind of dialogue that Rosenzweig advocated and of the limitations that he placed on the purposes of dialogue that Rosenstock-Huessy described their relationship as that of an "anvil and hammer."[5] For the dialogue between Rosenstock-Huessy and Rosenzweig rings with the forthright expression of men who are committed to positions which they believe to be "irreconcilable" within any historical time. There *is* a bond between anvil and hammer — together they forge an opposition to paganism, relativism, and indifference — but it is a bond wrought through the attraction of elements which are (in many ways) opposed to one another.

Rosenzweig has been praised for his remarkable openness to Christianity. The basis of that praise lies in his assertion that both Christianity and Judaism are "true religions." Such an acknowledgment should make possible Rosenzweig's picture of everything a dialogue should be, but this is not, in fact, what happens. For the way in which Rosenzweig conceives of Judaism, the way he understands covenant, points to only a halfhearted belief in the existence of two covenants. In the final analysis, Rosenzweig is not unlike his colleague, Leo Baeck, for whom dialogue could be nothing more than an airing of ideas, not an exchange. Unlike Baeck, Rosenzweig has the desire and the means to go beyond the sociological concerns of dialogue, but he fails to do so. The reason for this, I believe, lies in his conception of Jewish relationality — his conception of what it means to be covenanted — and his lack of commitment to the truth value of Christianity.

The "New Thinking"

"Speech thinking" is what Rosenzweig calls dialogue and it is the "cure" for those disciplines of thought, philosophy and theology in particular, which have been felled by "*apoplexia philosophica*,"[6] that is, German idealism. Thought that is so diseased has the qualities of abstraction and timelessness; it professes completeness and lacks subjectivity. To one who hears it, it is tedious, monological, a dry-throated soliloquy of death. "In the old philosophy, 'thinking' means thinking for no one else and speaking to no one else (and here, if you prefer, you may substitute 'everyone' or the well-known 'all the world' for 'no one')." In contrast, the "New Thinking" which Rosenzweig proposes, requires the genuine presence of at least two true individuals; it is thought that is addressed to another and that awaits the response of that other. "Speaking means speaking to some one and thinking for some one . . . a quite definite some one, and he has not only ears, like 'all the world,' but also a mouth."[7] Assuming mutuality, subjectivity, and a real future, it is dependent upon listeners who spontaneously become speakers.

Speech, or more precisely, dialogue, is the method of the New Thinking, and its starting point is "experience." The sort of experience that Rosenzweig refers to is not the experience "of" anything; reality is not made up of fixed substances that can be isolated from or reduced to one another. Rather, reality is an "enduring process" in which the present is "born anew each instant, and each instant it dies." To the question, "What is the *essence* of life?" Rosenzweig answers, "Life 'is' not, it simply occurs."[8] Questions about essence are wrongheaded because they presuppose that there is something behind experience to which all can be reduced—one isolated, unchanging thing. Such questions are the symptoms of reasoning that is experientially unsound, of reasoning that can lead the individual into a "paralysis of artificial death."[9]

"Artificial death" is the gift of that philosophy which works to dull the sting of death by numbing individuality. Is the fear of death overcome when the individual takes his or her place in The Whole which dissolves the one? No, says Rosenzweig, death simply comes more "warmly recommended" by philosophy. "We don't want a Philosophy that moves in the train of Death and tries to distract us from its perennial dominion by the harmony of her dance."[10] There is no cure for death. But the "narrowness of life" which afflicts the isolated individual can be treated, not by means of philosophical idealism which merely "mocks" the individual, but by a philosophy that affirms the individual as one irreducible fact whose existence can only be understood in reference to other irreducible facts.

Philosophy that is based on experience recognizes the standing claim of "common sense": that God, the World, and the Individual are the "first and last subjects of all philosophizing."[11] These are the irreducible elements of real experience. The fact that they are not interchangeable—that, for example, neither the divine nor the human individual can be dissolved into the World— does not preclude the fact that they *are* interrelated. Indeed, the relationship between the three elements of reality is "the experience of factuality that precedes all facts of real experience"; experience is itself relational.

> . . . the little word "and" [is] the basic word of all experience, the word the philosopher's tongue is not used to. God *and* the world *and* man! This "and" was the beginning of experience and so it must recur in the ultimate aspect of truth. For there must be an "and" within truth itself, within ultimate truth that can only be *one*.[12]

The key to overcoming the narrowness of life without prematurely destroying the individual is to embrace that which embraces us — to become conscious of the interrelatedness of God *and* the World *and* the Individual.

> . . . certainty of being "something" is not achieved by plumbing the depths of such an entity, but rather by opening the floodgates and permitting the stream of which it is a part to inundate it.[13]

There is no "something" in abstraction from the stream of life. To be "something" means to be in "context," literally to be woven together with the other parts of reality.

In *Understanding the Sick and the Healthy*, Rosenzweig exposes his hypothetical patient, a sufferer of German idealism, to the "environmental treatment" as the only means of chasing away the ghosts created by abstraction and recovering the concrete wholeness of life. Fundamental to this treatment is the position that while God, the World, and the Individual are "all equally transcendent in regard to each other," "God, man, and the world reveal themselves only in their relations to one another, that is, in creation, revelation, and redemption."[14] God-Individual-World signify the three points of one triangle; Creation-Revelation-Redemption signify the three points of another. When overlapped, the two triangles form the six-pointed "Star of Redemption," the visual model of the New Thinking. Linking the points into an ordered form are the lines that represent the interrelationship of each with all. Creation, revelation, and redemption are not single events which can be plotted on a time line; they are the unceasing and interconnected processes which define all life. It is in the ongoing dialogue between God, the Individual, and the World that the barest word becomes a meaningful story.

It is the connective "and" that stands in defiance to the reductive "one" of the Old Thinking. Where before there had been the solitary sounds of thought, now there was a many-voiced dialogue. Where before the singleness of continuity had reigned, now both continuity *and* novelty could flourish. Where before the future was indistinguishable from the past, now the future could be hoped for, anticipated, but not known until after it was given. Reality, as the "speaking speaker" understands it, is incomprehensible to the "thinking thinker." The former exchanges timeless thought for unfinished, because yet unmade, conversation. The speaking speaker "lives by virtue of another's life."

> . . . I do not know in advance what the other person will say to me, because I do not even know what I myself am going to say. . . . To require time means that we cannot anticipate, that we must wait for everything, *that what is ours depends on what is another's*.[15]

For Rosenzweig, dialogue is the best description of the process of life because it exemplifies that process. Like all life, dialogue seeks to overcome the power of the past, "to transcend the law which constitutes causation,"[16] and to be continually revitalized. It is the future which offers up newly-born moments as a replacement for that which is perpetually perishing. "In actual conversation something happens," and what happens is life itself.[17]

Judaism Despite Christianity: A Case Study in Dialogue

What happens when the ideal dialogue of the New Thinking is given the particular content of Jewish-Christian dialogue? In the correspondence between Rosenzweig and Rosenstock-Huessy we have a ready-made case study.

"We don't want to be philosophers when we are philosophizing, but human beings," writes Rosenzweig in a letter to Rosenstock-Huessy, "and so we must bring our philosophy into the form of our humanity."[18] In authentic dialogue the philosopher-as-human-being finds his or her real voice, the voice of a concrete individual speaking in full subjectivity. The letters of Rosenzweig and Rosenstock-Huessy provide us with the record of a hard-headed, sustained exchange between two philosophically sophisticated, existentially oriented, religiously committed "speech thinkers" who do not agree. What comes of this dialogue, what "happens" in their conversation? The disappointing and ironic fact is that although both participants hold to the metaphysics of the New Thinking, their conversation never generates the power they believe lies in real dialogue, power that is transformative. In the course of their interaction, neither Rosenzweig nor Rosenstock-Huessy is significantly transformed; they remain hammer and anvil. Nor does the contact between them succeed in changing the pitch of the sound they produce. It is sharp, loud, and all too consistent.

In the language of the New Thinking, what happens between Rosenzweig and Rosenstock-Huessy, or what doesn't happen, can be attributed to the loss of that which contributes "vital reality" to the language of experience: the "and." There are, according to Rosenzweig, three "archetypal" words of experience, but the first two — "yea" and "nay" — require the third — "and" — for their context. "And" is the "keystone of the arch of the substructure over which the edifice of the *logos* of linguistic sense is erected."[19] The "and" makes language meaningful because it is the expression of our basic intuition about reality itself. It is the "and" that is absent in the exchange between Rosenzweig and Rosenstock-Huessy. The positions they hold, their personal conceptions of Judaism and Christianity, are elaborated for one another — the "yea" and the "nay" are given. But the "and" that makes "what is ours depend[ent] on what is another's" is only superficially apparent. Thus what might have been an exemplary case of dialogue is instead an exemplary example of two individuals "witnessing" to their faiths.

Rosenzweig believes that Jews and Christians have an "obligation to understand" one another. A certain level of appreciation and an equal degree of tolerance follows from such understanding. But Rosenzweig makes it clear that the duty to understand another's faith and the duty to attempt to change it are incongruent. The missionary character of Christianity "throttle[s] the obligation to understand," and thus it is an intolerant religion. Judaism, in contrast, is "naturally tolerant" of other people both because it "promises 'eternal bliss to the pious of all people'" and because it does not engage in missionary activity.[20] Understanding breeds tolerance and tolerance excludes all efforts to change another religion. For Rosenzweig, the goal of any exchange between Jews and Christians is not change, but understanding.

Rosenzweig makes an important shift in his evaluation of "change" when the discussion turns from general metaphysics to missionary work. In his outline of the general nature of reality, Rosenzweig understands creation as the ongoing process which renews itself because it never ceases its creative activity. It is an affirmation of time; indeed, it endows time with meaning. Change, novelty, the future—these are fundamentals of reality; they are the zest of life. When the creative process of life is personalized, it becomes, in Rosenzweig's terminology, revelation. For Rosenzweig, what is revealed is not a past fact but a present reality. In revelation, God speaks to the individual as a "Thou" to a "Thou," as one immediate presence to another. Again, it is the spontaneity and the open-endedness of speech that captures the spirit of the reality envisioned by Rosenzweig.

When Rosenzweig takes up the topic of interfaith relations, however, he sets aside his positive valuation of change and replaces it with the Aristotelian notion that change is a process which implies deficiency. Missionary activity assumes the need for change among those to whom the mission is brought. In Rosenzweig's understanding, the missionary must assume that the duties being performed will result in that which is lesser—non-Christian traditions—becoming that which is greater—Christianity. Missionary activity is legitimate activity when dealing with those faiths which are lacking in religious truth. To be tolerant of such traditions is to be tolerant of those who are ignorant or that which is false. In this case, tolerance is not a virtue. The relationship between the proselyter and the would-be proselyte is not one of understanding, but one of change. For Rosenzweig, religious tolerance and missionary work are at odds.

It is Rosenzweig's position, however, that the Christian "obligation to missionize" takes precedence over the "obligation to understand" when the circumstances involve non-Jewish faiths. At the root of this position is his belief that only Judaism and Christianity are indeed religions. All other faiths are forms of paganism which, while not devoid of religious insight and feeling, are prereligions insofar as they lack a relationship with God gained through revelation.

> Paganism is no more, no less than truth itself, but truth reduced to its elements, invisible and unrevealed truth. So that whenever paganism sets out to represent the whole instead of an element, the form instead of the invisible, revelation instead of the unrevealed, it becomes a lie.[21]

Pagan traditions have "forgotten or denied" the revelation that was bestowed on Adam and thereby on humanity in general. Nevertheless, the pagan is not denied salvation. The rites of paganism may be "nothing but stupendous error," yet the prayers of individuals have not gone unheard.

> Did God wait for Mount Sinai or, perhaps, Golgotha? No paths that lead from Sinai and Golgotha are guaranteed to lead to him, but neither can he possibly have failed to come to one who sought him on the trails skirting Olympus. . . . There is . . . no block of wood in which he may not once take up his dwelling, and no psalm of David that will always reach his ear.[22]

In regards to "paganism," Rosenzweig upholds the classic Jewish doctrine that God grants salvation to "the pious among the nations," while the pagan tradition in itself is not acknowledged to be a valid agency of salvation. "For the voice of one living God echoes only where there is life, even if that life be intoxicated with gods and hostile to God."[23]

Because non-Jewish, non-Christian traditions operate without cognizance of divine revelation, the truth they do possess as beneficiaries of the continuous creation is unintegrated and therefore easily tempted into idolatry. There is something artificial, "founded," about these other faiths[24], the result of their being bound to the level of humanity or nature. Of the "good Turk" [the Moslem], Rosenzweig writes that he "has more in common with Goethe . . . than with either Jew or Christian."

> He doesn't know, and cannot know, the quite otherworldly attitude of the soul that yet breathes the world with every breath, an attitude that is peculiar to religion within revelation (because only revelation means that overshadowing of the world by another world, which is the objective presupposition of that attitude of the soul.)[25]

Rosenzweig rejects the idea that Islam has the same sort of relationship with Judaism that Christianity does. So thoroughly does he disregard Islam's own self-understanding that he unflinchingly asserts that it is a "remarkable case of plagiarism in world history," insofar as it is based on revelation imparted not

by God, but "derived directly from paganism." The way of Allah is no transcendent path, according to Rosenzweig, but simply a series of all too human
acts.[26]

In a similar manner he disposes of Buddhism, Hinduism, and Taoism.
Their efforts to dissolve the particular into the universal distort the real relations that exist between the irreducible elements of reality. If the world and the
individual are mere illusions, then it is not possible to talk meaningfully about
creation, revelation, redemption, or relationships between actual individuals;
nor is it possible to maintain the relationships which characterize a truly
religious perspective — those between the Creator and the creation, the
Revealer and the receiver, and the Redeemer and the redeemed.

What all non-Jewish, non-Christian traditions share is their inadequate
understanding of or sensitivity to divine revelation, and consequently, their
understandings of creation and redemption are unsatisfactory. For creation,
revelation, and redemption are not separate processes that occur in isolation
from one another: they are in fact, all the same — the process in which God
loves the world and the individual and in which the individual responds to that
love. Although no one part of the process is less essential than another part,
there is a sense in which revelation is the linchpin. In revelation, general
truths of creation are addressed to the individual, who is called upon to act in
light of these truths. What the individual is called to do is to "love the nighest,"
the neighbor, and this love becomes the individual's personal testament to God
and to the love which God has for the creation. In loving the neighbor and
thereby returning love to the Lover, the response to revelation becomes an act
of redemption.

Traditions, then, that do not hear the voice of revelation cannot fully appreciate the acts of creation or fully participate in the acts of redemption. There is
no unity to the lives of those communities. Without a sense of the interconnectedness of all life (as represented by the overlapping triangles of the Star),
these communities have no real redemptive power and leave their members
with the choice either to live without any ultimate meaning or to provide
meaning by raising that which is not ultimate to the level of ultimacy. It is this
second option that is most often chosen, and that is the reason why the insights
of paganism become distorted into idolatry. To these communities the Christian mission is rightfully an advocate of change, calling upon the individual to
move from the inadequate, the false, and the pseudo-religious into a truly
religious life.

The Relationship between Judaism and Christianity

It is the invalidity of the pagan traditions as religions that legitimates missionary efforts, but the situation is entirely otherwise when two valid religions
meet. In the encounter between two tenable religions, the impulse to convert

is replaced by the desire to understand, the purpose of such an encounter being to reach a level of understanding that will yield both theological and sociological tolerance. The participants take each other's claims seriously — seriously enough to put aside all missionary activity, but not so seriously as to transform one's own religion in light of the other.

The encounter between Judaism and Christianity is the encounter between "the two distinct historical manifestations of revelation"[27] — that is, the only two genuine religious faiths. The similarity between Judaism and Christianity hinges on this common grounding in the revelatory word of God and, consequently, their fundamental antagonism toward paganism and "natural religion."

> This common religion, quite real, is the human aspect of the common objective origin of revelation, also quite real, just as the complementary contrast between their saints is the human aspect of the objective oneness of the two faiths, a oneness determined by a common goal. Hence the common distinction of this religious life from all that stands outside revelation (or puts itself outside).[28]

But although Judaism and Christianity share a common origin and goal (and common opponents as well), although they are two coins minted of the same "metal," they are not the same coin.[29] To describe the uniqueness of the relationship between Judaism and Christianity, Rosenzweig forges a middle way "between complete identity and absolute opposition."[30]

This middle way is the means by which Rosenzweig attempts a solution to one of the sorest problems of modern religious thought — how to escape religious absolutism yet avoid religious relativism — and to answer one of its most pressing questions: what, if any, is the place of Judaism in the modern world? What Rosenzweig argues is that the relationship between the two genuine religions is the paradoxical one of complementarity and polarity. In their worst antagonist they find their best complement. Though they are different historical expressions of the truth given in revelation, they are both valid expressions. Thus the reason for much of the strife that has existed between the two faiths lies in the tendency to disregard the complementary parts of their natures; each sees itself as the only valid faith and mistakes the other for a pagan form. In fact, Rosenzweig argues, they stand together against a mutual external foe. In a letter to Rosenstock-Huessy, Rosenzweig asserts:

> That which abides [after the sacrifices of Moriah and Golgotha] is different; on the one hand an external community, and on the other an external man — and the consequences of this make mutual understanding so difficult that the one side is always being seduced into classifying the other with those that know of nothing abiding [that is, paganism].[31]

Judaism and Christianity must recognize that they are dependent on one another if the enemy is to be vanquished. They own different weapons, each necessary but neither sufficient without the other. In the fight to overcome paganism, victory is the premium of cooperation.

Rosenzweig supplies a standard against which the variety of world faiths can be measured, thereby avoiding the horn of relativism. He finds two faiths which meet the standard, yet which cannot claim self-sufficiency, and thus he avoids the horn of absolutism. By naming Judaism as one of only two valid religions and conceiving of these two religions as adverse to one another and yet indebted to one another, Rosenzweig marks out a clear place for German Jewry. Whether Rosenzweig does this by proposing that there are two equally valid, equally sufficient covenants — one between God and the Jews, the other between God and the Christians — is the topic under consideration in the remainder of this chapter.

The Eternal People and Eternal Life

Between the year 1906, when he was twenty years old, and the year 1916, when he was thirty, Rosenzweig's personal commitment to and understanding of Judaism underwent a radical change. In a diary entry dated March, 1906, Rosenzweig enumerates the bases of his Judaism:

1. "It is the religion of my forefathers" . . .
2. "I enjoy observing certain customs without having any real reason for doing so."
3. "I believe in Plato." . . .
4. "I like to think in terms of biblical images." . . . Of these pillars, 1 is the central and strongest; 2 is a circle of slenderer columns that support the periphery of the temple roof; 3 and 4 are pilasters, strong enough in themselves, but in this particular edifice service only as ornaments.[32]

Rosenzweig's primary reason for being a Jew is based on "nationalism," on the coincidence of parentage. He terms his second reason "metaphysical" or dogmatic, "since the ceremonial law is in a sense our dogma." The third and fourth reasons fall into the categories of "eudaemonist moods" and "a disposition toward myth-making," respectively.[33]

This set of justifications, Rosenzweig soon realizes, is not a very robust program for either remaining Jewish or returning to Judaism. When his cousin, Hans Ehrenberg, decides to convert to Christianity in 1909, Rosenzweig writes his parents:

> We are Christian in everything. We live in a Christian state . . . in short, our
> whole "culture" rests entirely on a Christian foundation; consequently a man
> who has nothing holding him back needs only a very slight push . . . to make
> him accept Christianity.[34]

In 1913, following an intense discussion on religion with Rosenstock-Huessy, it became clear to Rosenzweig that his reasons for remaining nominally Jewish were insubstantial. Aside from his enjoyment of Plato and biblical imagery, which have a place in Christianity as well, Rosenzweig's Judaism appeared to be mere sentimentality, not real religion at all. For one who believed that a religious orientation was essential to an individual's life, baptism seemed to be the only viable alternative.

But Rosenzweig's conclusion was annulled during what was to be his last Yom Kippur service before becoming a Christian. Although Rosenzweig never spoke directly about what happened to him during the service, it is clear that he left the synagogue able to make a confession of faith from within Judaism. The experience was the cornerstone of Rosenzweig's future work; the "reasoning process" by which he built his experience into a modern form of Judaism occupied the rest of Rosenzweig's intellectual life.

The basis of Rosenzweig's new understanding, unlike that of his earlier Judaism, is metaphysical and theological. He summarizes it in a letter to Rosenstock-Huessy:

> (1) That we have the truth, (2) that we are at the goal, and (3) that any and every
> Jew feels in the depth of his soul that Christian relation to God, and so in a sense
> their religion, is particularly and extremely pitiful, poverty-stricken, and cere-
> monious; namely, that as a Christian one has to learn from someone else,
> whoever he may be, to call God "our Father." To the Jew, that God is our Father
> is the first and most self-evident fact — and what need is there for a third person
> between me and my father in Heaven? That is no discovery of modern apolo-
> getics but the simplest Jewish instinct, a mixture of failure to understand and
> pitying contempt.[35]

The core of these three articles is the same: the centrality of relationship. Having the truth and being at the goal are two ways of describing the ultimate human relationship with God. The goal of religion is to speak the Truth that becomes "truth for someone,"[36] that is truth by which the individual can live even in the face of death. Such truth is embodied in those religious forms which anticipate eternity and thereby dissolve the dominion of death. That which anticipates eternity is already at the goal; in such truth it knows redemption. A religion that is at the goal is a religion that realizes the immediate interconnectedness of the three life processes — creation, revelation, and redemption — and the three subjects of life — God, humanity, and the world. It is life whose pattern is the "Star of Redemption."

For Rosenzweig, it is this experience of relational immediacy between the individual and God that characterizes Judaism and that distinguishes it from Christianity. In the face of this experience, dogmatic affirmations and debates about essences are disruptive noises. "There is no 'essence of Judaism,' there is only: 'Hear O Israel!' "[37] "Hear O Israel!" is the call to relationship and in the dialogue which follows, the individual Jew establishes the terms of his or her relationship with God. The call to relationship with God is not only revelatory but also redemptive. The moment in which the people of Israel listened is the moment in which eternity was written in their hearts.

The experience of relational immediacy that is expressed in the liturgy as "Hear O Israel!" has its life in the "fact of the Jewish people." At Sinai and in every moment thereafter, the Jews constituted themselves as a "we." In response to that which was imparted and communicated, they formed the framework for ongoing participation, community. This community, this people, is the "visible form by whose means they [the Jews] wrest their eternity from time."[38] In the people of Israel there is no longer any contradiction between creation and revelation because redemption has become transparent. It is in the Jewish people that eternity — the promise of redemption — has a home in the present. It is because the Jewish people form a perfect community that eternity is both anticipated by it and realized within it.

> [The Jew] does not have to wait for world history to unroll its long course to let him gain what he feels he already possesses in the circuit of every year: *the experience of the immediacy of each single individual to God, realized in the perfect community of all with God.*[39]

For Rosenzweig, it is the fact of the Jewish people that is the expression of Judaism's ultimacy as a religion.

The notion of election and the idea that eternity is a present reality in the Jewish people are one and the same. Indeed, Rosenzweig rarely employs the traditional appellation, "chosen people," speaking instead of the Jews as the "eternal people."[40]

Like the medieval Jewish thinker, Judah Halevi, Rosenzweig starts with the fact of the Jewish people. His discussion focuses on the consequences of this fact for the people itself and for the whole of humanity, not the events which preceded it. No causal connection is made between the behavior of the community which received revelation and the fact that revelation was given to it. In this, Rosenzweig is consonant with that part of Jewish tradition which affirms the spontaneous, arbitrary nature of God's revelation at Sinai. *That* the Jewish people is, not how it came to be, is his concern.

> "We are what we are, but we are Jews," runs the catch of a little Galician song with unsurpassably illogical logic — "but," not "therefore."[41]

The Jewish people is defined, above all, by its sheer existence.

The prerevelatory history of the Israelites is not remarkable. It is the moment when eternity penetrated history, when this assembly became a community, that is extraordinary. At that moment, when the Israelites became a community under revelation, they entered the Kingdom and, paradoxically, gave reality to the Kingdom. Time, for this people, is no longer the relationship between past and future; it is the relationship between the Kingdom that has come and the Kingdom that will come. This people now lives from within a "future which without ceasing to be future is nevertheless present."[42]

To experience eternity or redemption, to live in the Kingdom and in hopes of the Kingdom, is to be elected. In the life of the Jewish people, the future bears witness to the past, which is to say that the redemptive future is already the possession of this people.

> Eternity is just this: that time no longer has a right to a place between the present moment and consummation, and that the whole future is to be grasped today.[43]

The Jewish people is the Eternal People in a double sense: Time is not descriptive of Jewish relationships because in its witness to the eternal, Jewish life has become nontemporal life. The power of Judaism lies in its ahistorical or "metahistorical" nature—only that which lives outside of time can truly represent that which is timeless.

The notion of Jewish timelessness or eternality has several important implications for Rosenzweig's conception of Judaism. First, there is the idea that the destiny of the Jewish people has been determined once and for all by the first generation, the Sinai generation. Love for God, once born, becomes an element in the people's life that is "static, a constant."[44] Rosenzweig insures the constancy of this love over the generations by translating theology into biology.

> There is only one community . . . which cannot utter the "we" of its unity without hearing deep within a voice that adds: "are eternal." It must be a blood-community, because only blood gives present warrant to the hope for a future. . . . Only a community based on common blood feels the warrant of eternity warm in its veins even now.[45]

Rosenzweig advances a version of the traditional birth dogma of chosenness. "Shall I 'be converted' when I have been 'chosen' from birth?" he asks his friend Rosenstock-Huessy.[46] While conversion is not theologically necessary, it is also not biologically possible. There is one route to becoming a Jew, a route which overlaps with the biological process of embryogenesis. And there is no route by which one can take leave of one's destiny. "A soul that thinks it can say *no* to its destiny will find out that it isn't free but simply naked."[47]

Secondly, the idea of timelessness is strengthened, and the necessity for biological inheritance as well, by Rosenzweig's position that the Jewish people is "in" the world but not "of" it.[48] Jews are in the world only as witnesses to the generations which preceded them, as witnesses to their blood relations. The purpose of the Jewish people is to *live* and to reproduce, and thereby to ensure the continued historical presence of the eternal revelation. The fulfillment of this duty requires that the existence of the Jewish people not be tied to any conditional reality, to any historical form which might claim the loyalty that is reserved for existence itself. To this purpose the Eternal People refuses the garments that other people wear to distinguish themselves as communal entities: land, language, and laws and customs set down by temporal powers. The land for which the Eternal People yearns is not a nation-state but a "holy land"; the language of the Jews is not a language of politics and markets, but a "holy language"; and the laws and customs by which the Jews abide are not fluid and mutable, but eternally valid. To wear the robe of eternity is to discard all accoutrements of temporality.

> And so, in the final analysis, it [this people] is not alive in the sense the nations are alive: in a national life manifest on this earth, in a national territory, solidly based and staked out on the soil. It is alive only in that which guarantees it will endure beyond time, in that which pledges it everlastingness, in drawing its own eternity from the sources of the blood.[49]

For the Jewish people, biology is not modified by postrevelation history; it is magnified.

Thirdly, Rosenzweig describes Judaism as the fire that burns at the core of the star, at the center of the matrix of life. In this metaphor, Judaism's eternality is again stressed.

> The fire of the core must burn incessantly. Its flame must eternally feed upon itself. It requires no fuel from without. Time has no power over it and must roll past. It must produce its own time and reproduce itself forever.[50]

Rosenzweig's description of Judaism here bears a surprising resemblance to the neo-Platonic description of the Eternal One. In having entered the realm of eternity, the fire that is Judaism "burns through and in itself."[51] In blazing beyond time, the flame glows without the aid of external relationships. It is self-sufficient, rekindling itself by its own heat. Moreover, and related to this, the flame renews itself but does not grow—all turning is a return home. It is precisely this self-sufficiency, this lack of relations, "this rooting in ourselves, and in nothing but ourselves, that vouchsafes eternity."[52]

Without hesitation Rosenzweig draws the logical conclusion that follows from this position.

What does this mean: to root in one's self? What does it mean that here one individual people does not seek the warrant of its existence in the external, and reaches out for eternity in its very lack of relations with the outside world? It means no more and no less than that one people, though it is only one people, claims to constitute All.[53]

Rosenzweig completes his picture of Judaism with an assertion of Jewish absolutism. In so doing, both the theory of the New Thinking and the method it gave rise to—dialogue—are undercut.

Two related questions of significance need yet to be explored: the question of Jewish efficacy in the world and the question of the necessity and value of Christianity. First, how is it that Rosenzweig can hold that a relationship of immediacy with God can be maintained apart from any relations with external reality? The problem is especially pressing because Rosenzweig maintains that the commandment to love God can only be fulfilled by loving one's neighbor. Secondly, how can Rosenzweig maintain that Christianity is a necessary complement to Judaism? In what sense are the two faiths interdependent if Judaism is self-sufficient and complete?

Christianity: The Eternity of Realization

Had "failure to understand" and "pitying contempt"[54] been Rosenzweig's last words on Christianity, Rosenzweig's theological legacy would have been much diminished. But in fact, in his unique understanding of Christianity, Rosenzweig turns in the opposite direction from pity and contempt toward respect and appreciation. Beyond that, he makes the significant move toward a degree of mutual dependency between Judaism and Christianity.

Rosenzweig's sympathy for Christianity, however, rarely extends beyond the instrumental value that Christianity has for Judaism. Christianity is the vehicle by which Judaism finds worldwide acceptance; it is the means of Jewish efficacy in the events of history. Finally, for Rosenzweig, Christianity's value is primarily instrumental and only minimally intrinsic. It is this understanding of Christianity which foils the possibility that the Jewish role in dialogue will be anything more than that of witness.

The Intrinsic Value of Christianity

Rosenzweig's positive evaluation of Christianity has been acclaimed by numerous Christian thinkers as the ground for the modern discussion of Jewish-Christian relations. His approach is favorably viewed by Christians as a "breakthrough to real dialogue,"[55] and conversely, his recognition of Christian claims has often been assessed with suspicion by Jewish thinkers.

The common ground of Judaism and Christianity extends beyond that which Rosenzweig attributes to the various forms of paganism — that is, beyond the recognition that salvation is universally available to the pious among the nations. Unlike paganism, which reflects the "secret premises of ever renewed reality" and hence exhibits its participation in the divine creative process, Judaism and Christianity are the two "forms that eternally reflect a reality eternally renewed."[56] It is because they are formed by revelation that Judaism and Christianity reflect eternity. And insofar as they are products of revelation they are both valid religions. In this way Rosenzweig accords Christianity an independent significance; its validity is rooted in revelation and is not dependent upon any normative determinations made by Judaism.

Judaism and Christianity differ in the "external, visible forms by whose means they wrest eternity from time." The "fact" of the Jewish people is the Jewish form of eternity; its parallel in Christianity is the "event" that is the life of Jesus.[57] Rosenzweig regards Judaism and Christianity as the "ultimate facts" and in doing so recognizes that he has transcended "the usual apologetics and polemics in the field — probably for the first time."[58]

The strongest assertion of parity between Judaism and Christianity issues from Rosenzweig's theory of truth. Within the parameters of the New Thinking, truth is relational, validated in life, and known by the individual only partially.

> Unlike the truth of the philosophers, which is not allowed to know anything but itself, this truth must be truth for some one. If it is to be the one truth, it can be only for the One, God. And that is why our truth must of necessity become manifold, and why "the" truth must be converted into "our" truth. Thus truth ceases to be what "is" true and becomes a verity that wants to be verified, realized in active life.[59]

The New Thinking promotes an understanding of truth as that which becomes true only within the concrete experience of human life. Sometimes verification is attained only in the sacrifice of an individual's life, and sometimes the sacrifice of generations of lives is required for verification. Never does verification encompass the whole truth, for that is God's possession alone. What it means to be human is to have a personal portion of the eternal; truth has been "im-parted" to humanity. To God's Truth which is One, humankind speaks the word, "Truly," a word which reflects the fragmentary and subjective portion of the truth that is humanity's.[60]

Such a theory of truth "replaces the old theories of non-contradiction and objects, and introduces a dynamic for the old static concept of objectivity." Although he prefers not to label his position, Rosenzweig finds the tag, "absolute empiricism," most descriptive, partly because it fits "the attitude that claims to know nothing more of the divine than it has experienced . . . and nothing more of terrestrial matters than it has experienced."[61]

From this theory of truth, Rosenzweig is able to affirm the truth of Christianity as well as the truth of Judaism. Like all human knowledge, these truths are partial and the expression of their partial nature is the contradiction arising from the two claims. There is no human way to resolve the contradiction, for verification in history is also only partial. Each religion speaks truth, but neither speaks the Truth in its wholeness. It is not possible, according to Rosenzweig, to aver anything more than this.

> . . . this messianic theory of knowledge that values truths according to what it has cost to verify them, and according to the bond they create among men, cannot lead beyond the two eternally irreconcilable hopes for the Messiah: the hope for one to come and the hope for one to return; it cannot lead beyond the "and" of these final efforts in behalf of truth. Beyond this, only God can verify the truth, and for him only is there only one truth.[62]

The preceding discussion constitutes a solid basis for the claim that Rosenzweig affirms a Christian as well as a Jewish covenant and that in so doing, he initiates an interfaith dialogue that is open, mutually appreciative, and potentially transformative. If the truth that each individual possesses is only partial and if different individuals possess different truths, then both a "why" and a "to what ends" of dialogue are given. Moreover, and related, Rosenzweig seems to affirm that Christianity is intrinsically valuable as a religion based on revealed truth. It is valuable apart from its relationship to Judaism.

The Instrumental Value of Christianity:
Christianity in the Service of Judaism

There is, however, much in Rosenzweig's discussion which serves to weaken his apparently wholehearted affirmation of the parity between Judaism and Christianity. Numerous statements disrupt this picture of equality between the two faiths. The weight of these statements in Rosenzweig's thought exceeds that given to those statements in which Rosenzweig affirms Christian-Jewish parity.

It is the New Thinking that, among other things, enables Rosenzweig to defy absolutism and to declare himself in favor of a pluralism of revealed religions. In particular, it is the New Thinking that opens a way for Rosenzweig to pronounce with vigor and conviction his allegiance to Judaism. However, in pursuing the possibilities made available to him by this initial insight, Rosenzweig returns to the principles of thought which had obstructed his way in the beginning—the historical absolutism of Hegelian thought. The

New Thinking, with its emphasis on relationality and its orientation to the future is mostly forgotten by Rosenzweig when he describes the "hyper-cosmos." Judaism is the metahistorical and self-sufficient expression of eter-nity on which all other faiths, including Christianity, are dependent. Judaism is the embodiment of that anticipation for which all faiths hope. In the final analysis, Judaism *is* what other religions yearn, mostly unconsciously, to become. In Hegelian terms, it is the ideal that is really real.

There are two major metaphors by which Rosenzweig conceptualizes the relationship between Judaism and Christianity: the seed and the branch and the fire and its rays. The fundamental inferiority of Christianity to Judaism is at the heart of each one. The metaphor of the seed and the branch figures prominently in Rosenzweig's discussion and does much to damage the argu-ment for parity between the faiths. It is borrowed from the medieval Jewish thinker, Judah Halevi, and Rosenzweig quotes it in its entirety at the end of his discussion of Christianity in *The Star of Redemption.*

> "Thus God has a secret plan for us, a plan like his plan for a seed-grain which drops into the ground and appears to change into earth and water and dirt, till nothing remains of it by which the eye might recognize it; and which nonetheless transforms earth and water into its own essence, which decomposes their ele-ments step by step and converts and adapts them to its own material, till it produces bark and leaves; and once its inner marrow is prepared to receive the embryo of the former seed for new corporeality, the tree produces fruit like that whence the seed first came: thus the law of Moses draws every successor in its train, transforming him in reality even though to all appearances everyone rejects it. And the nations are the readying and preparation of the Messiah whom we await. He will be the fruit, and all will become his fruit and acknowl-edge him, and the tree will be one. Then they will praise and glorify the root which once they despised, of which Isaiah spoke."[63]

The above discussion and its further elaboration are placed under the heading, "The Realization of Eternity." Judaism as the seed is eternity implanted in the world, and as the fruit it is redemption universally realized. As the branch of the tree, Christianity is merely the temporary physical structure which sup-ports the process; it is neither the necessary nor the sufficient part. The force that drives the fruit from its leaves is other than the branch itself. Christianity is the "way" but it is not the "life." Indeed, Rosenzweig asserts that "the truth lies *behind* the way," and he continues, "the way ends when home has been reached."[64] Christianity is an instrument for attaining this end. But the end itself is Judaism.

The second metaphor, the fire and its rays, is only slightly more generous in its depiction of Christianity. Christianity is symbolized as the rays which emanate from the fire that is Judaism. To the Jew, God gave eternal life by "kindling the fire of the Star of his truth in our hearts." To the Christian was given the eternal way, guided by "the rays of that Star of his truth for all time unto the eternal end."[65] The rays are in a direct sense the light unto the nations—they illuminate God's truth for those as yet unresponsive to revelation. As Judaism is both eternity anticipated and the anticipation of eternity, Christianity is, for the non-Jew, both the way to truth and eternally on the way to truth. While in Judaism it is life that is eternal—the fire burns incessantly, in Christianity it is the way that is eternal—in the light shed by the rays, an endless path is irradiated.

Although in this metaphor there is a certain degree of interdependence, the exchange is not symmetrical. While the fire depends on the rays for its effectiveness, for the extension of itself, the rays depend on the fire for their very life. "Judaism . . . is the One Nucleus whose glow provides invisible nourishment to the rays."[66] In discussing the relationship of fire to rays, the theory of truth which had enabled Rosenzweig to affirm Christian truth is qualified. Although he still maintains that Judaism and Christianity have a common goal—the redemption of the world—an asymmetrical relationship emerges from the metaphor.

There *is* an intimacy between the two that proves their common cause. Christianity is indebted to Judaism for the content of its message. The truth which Christianity preaches is a disguised version of the truth already alive within Judaism. Conversely, Judaism is indebted to Christianity for the form by which the message is made accessible to the pagan world. For "life" cannot be taught to another—it cannot be objectified; it is what one is born into. One can, however, be instructed in that which is exemplified in dogma and creed—in the "way"—and hence the non-Jew can be shown the path to truth through the baptismal ceremonies of missionary Christians. That which is eternal in itself, the Jewish people, knows not the "way" to eternity—it "is" while all others are "becoming"—and hence requires the aid of those who are on the way in order to be effective in the world. Christianity is the bearer of that truth which is lived by the Jewish people and which inspires Christianity. But it is only the beast of burden, the messenger. Judaism is the spiritual bearer, the parent "ever unrecognized by the nations" who bore "that prophecy which the nations had to believe, already fulfilled in the vicarious suffering of the individual for the individuals."[67] Christianity is the means by which the world is made to understand the way to redemption. It is the instrument of that which already lives in eternity, Judaism. Judaism and Christianity complement one another, but they are not symmetrical: Judiasm is intrinsically valuable while Christianity is only instrumentally valuable.

As the instrument of Judaism, Christianity has its life in the pagan world, to whom it can speak because in its "blood" it is pagan.

This is, in fact, the profoundest difference between Jewish and Christian man: the Christian is by nature or at least by birth — a pagan; the Jew, however, is a Jew. Thus the way of the Christian must be a way of self-externalization, of self-renunciation. . . . The life of the Jew, on the other hand, must precisely not lead him out of himself; he must rather live his way ever deeper into himself. The more he finds himself, the more he turns his back on paganism, which for him is on the outside not, as with the Christian, on the inside.[68]

Unlike the Jew who is born Jewish, the Christian must be baptized into Christianity. It is in Christ, not in themselves, that eternality is found.[69]

It is because of the paganism within Christianity that Christianity can conquer the world — it is truly *of* the world — and yet not attain the completeness which redemption brings. The Christian's flesh and blood are profaned, not just because the Christian dwells within the profane world, but because the Christian is corrupted by this world. In its quest for power, the Christian enters into compromise with the pagan. It is this compromising nature that diverts Christianity from the end and keeps it ever at the beginning of the way. The means by which the pagan people are "judaized"[70] is yet in constant turmoil with its own pagan roots.

For Rosenzweig, the Christian conception of the God-Man is the most telling example of the affinity between Christianity and paganism.

He [the Christian] cannot imagine that God himself, the holy God, could so condescend to him as he demands, except by becoming human himself. *The inextinguishable segment of paganism which is innermost in every Christian bursts forth here.* The pagan wants to be surrounded by human deities; he is not satisfied with being human himself: God too must be human.[71]

This belief, that God somehow became human in the life of Jesus, is central to Christianity. It is highly significant that Rosenzweig impugns this crucial theological doctrine, declaring it to be inextricably tied to paganism and hence to irreligion. Here it becomes especially clear that the conversion from paganism to Christianity is not enough, that there must be something beyond Christianity which corrects it and completes it. That something is, in Rosenzweig's system, Judaism.

The existence of the Jew constantly subjects Christianity to the idea that it is not attaining the goal, the truth, that it ever remains — on the way. That is the profoundest reason for the Christian hatred of the Jew, which is heir to the pagan hatred of the Jew. . . . it is hatred of one's own imperfection, one's own not-yet.[72]

As the "louse in the fur" of Christianity,[73] Judaism drives Christianity to the realization that despite its worldly power, it is incomplete, dependent, and ever in danger of losing its way. "By radiating apart to the outside, Christianity threatens to lose itself in individual rays far from the divine nucleus of truth." It is the existence of the Jewish people that not only keeps Christianity on the way, but most significantly, actually "stands surety for their [Christian] truth."[74]

Precisely because Christianity is "a living effectiveness of truth," that is, the worldwide network by which Jewish insights are disseminated, it does not know truth in the way known by Judaism. Neither of the religions, it is true, possesses the whole truth, but Rosenzweig deprives Christianity of the degree of truth he grants to Judaism.

> They [the Christians], for their part, run after the current of time, but the truth remains at their back; though led by it, since they follow its rays, they do not see it with their eyes. . . . they are denied a living view *altogether* for the sake of a living effectiveness of the truth.[75]

Christians see that which is irradiated by the rays emanating from the core of truth while Jews see the core or "star" itself.

Jews do not, however, see that which is illuminated by the light of Christianity. Nevertheless, what Rosenzweig denies the Jew — illuminative effectiveness — does not finally seem to be so much of a loss, and this for several reasons. Primarily, in Rosenzweig's mind, the Jews as a people have already arrived at the goal for which all other peoples yearn. Jews have "that inner unity of faith and life which . . . is still no more than a dream to the nations within the church." In perhaps the most important paradox that Rosenzweig frames, he asserts the unique characteristic of the Jewish people to be its ability to "bind creation as a whole to redemption while redemption is still to come." Although redemption means redemption-of-the-world, there is for Rosenzweig a sense in which redemption has occurred in a basically unredeemed world. The Jewish people has "reached the goal which it anticipates in hope."[76] Secondly, Rosenzweig maintains that the internal self-examination of the Jew cannot but yield universal benefits: At the interior of Judaism is the ultimate structure of existence — the essential interconnectedness of God, the World, and the Individual. In this understanding of reality, "the apparently exclusively-Jewish aspect of this threefold sentiment, apparently constricted and exclusive and isolated, now closes ranks again into the one all-illuminating stellar image of truth."[77]

There is one final way in which Rosenzweig qualifies his statements about Jewish loss of the world. Jewish art and theology, he argues, give the Jewish people a unity and a stability. The Jewish people is then able to "work as a ferment on Christianity and through it on the world."[78] The Jewish people does not lack relationships and hence efficacy in the world. In important ways, then, Christianity is "rendered irrelevant to Judaism."[79] "The fire is not aware of the rays nor does it have need of their light for itself."[80] There is no parity of value in this statement.

What then at various times appears to be an affirmation of two religious covenants, of the parity of value between Judaism and Christianity, finally does not have a secure place in Rosenzweig's system. There are not, for Rosenzweig, two "ways" *to* truth; there is one way *toward* truth—Christianity, and there is one life *in* truth—Judaism. The Hegelian dialectic which would have supported a two-covenant approach—Judaism as the thesis, Christianity as the antithesis, redemption of the world as the synthesis—does not hold. For Rosenzweig, Christianity is not truly Judaism's antithesis; instead, it is an efficacious tool of Judaism. More significantly, Rosenzweig maintains that redemption is possible only if Judaism is finally the only *kind* of redemptive power working within the world. "Where everything is on fire, there are no more rays, there is only one light."[81]

Very close to the end of *The Star of Redemption*, Rosenzweig writes that "it is the mouth by whose words man lives."[82] What are the words that a Jew who listens closely to Rosenzweig's words can speak in an encounter with a non-Jew? Despite Rosenzweig's strong advocacy of a new way of thinking established on principles that would make for genuine dialogue between real individuals, he describes a form of Judaism which is incongruent with these principles. Dialogue requires that the participants maintain an openness that applies to truth (at least in part) and to time (that is, a real future). But Rosenzweig's Judaism is self-sufficient—not fundamentally dependent on another human structure; it is essentially complete, static, temporally unambivalent, monolithic, and actually and wholly true (though not the whole truth). In contrast to the Jews, the people of the covenant, are those who are in the process of becoming covenanted to God but who never reach this goal in human history. There are not two covenants. There are those who are already *with* God and there are those who are on the way *to* God. To those who are on the eternal way, the Jewish witness to eternality is a light and a lamp. The transformative exchange which may occur is one-directional, extending from Judaism to Christianity and then to paganism.

Critical Reassessment

In a 1922 diary entry, Rosenzweig wrote about the influence of his friend, R. Nobel, on his life:

> Through him I have become more tolerant than I was formerly. Three years ago I was more orthodox, anti-Christian, anti-heretical than I am now. What I have learned from Nobel is that the soul of a *great* Jew can accommodate many things. There is danger only for the little souls.[83]

How great-souled Rosenzweig finally was able to be in regard to Jewish-Christian relations is questionable, however. Seen within the context of his generation, Rosenzweig deserves the praise he has received for moving beyond the traditional Jewish understanding of Christianity to a level of tolerance based on theological respect. In seeing Christianity as a positive means of achieving salvation for all non-Jews—as a "distinct historical manifestation of revelation"—he breaks through the Noachide paradigm in which Judaism is the only positive vehicle to salvation. In this way he succeeds in expanding the soul of Judaism.

It is Rosenzweig's conception of the complementary natures of the two religions—the idea that there is a third option between "complete identity and absolute opposition"—that transcends the nineteenth-century context of his thought and has significance for the current discussion of interfaith dialogue. Rosenzweig's sensitivity to the complexity of the relationship between the two faiths is apparent in the following diary entry:

> Jews and Christians both deny that the ethical and religious principle of "Love God and thy neighbor" is their common possession. Each tries to impute paganism to the other: the Christians by disallowing our love of neighbor, we by disallowing their love of God. Both are right and both wrong. Here the insincerity of liberal theology becomes apparent.[84]

"Both are right and both wrong"—here is the basis for dialogue that might open its participants to a deeper sense of the truth. In emphasizing complementarity rather than either extreme of commonality or opposition, Rosenzweig moves toward transformative dialogue.

He fails, however, to carry out the insights either of his theory of religion or of the method, the New Thinking, which supports his theory. The subordinate position of Christianity in Rosenzweig's picture of Judaism as the star and Christianity as the rays, or Judaism as eternal life and Christianity as the eternal way, is destructive of a truly complementary relationship. In Rosenzweig's view, Judaism needs no complement; it is complete and fulfilled apart from any relationship with Christianity. But Christianity (and all other faiths as well) depends on its relationship to Judaism, which is both the effective cause of Christianity—it generates Christianity's power in the world—and the final cause of Christianity—it is the goal toward which Christianity aims. The contrast between the two religions which had first elicited Rosenzweig's respect is lost in his systematic exposition of the relationship between the faiths. What had been appreciated as "diversities in contrast" becomes, in history, "diversities in opposition"[85] and ultimately, at the end of time, an untransformed singularity. Rosenzweig anticipates the coming together of all temporary religious modes into the permanent, eternal life of Judaism. Christianity is finally not the "ultimate fact" Rosenzweig had named it to be. It is Judaism alone that is "ultimate." The fruits of pluralism remain unsavored.

Apart from Rosenzweig's notion of complementarity, there is another opening in his thought which could yield stronger support for veridical pluralism. In the "New Thinking" and in his understanding of revelation, the common theme is relational immediacy. What happens between two speech-thinkers in dialogue and what happens in revelation is analogous: the presence of the one becomes known to the other. There is no formal content either of divine revelation or of human encounter; we meet commanding presences, but no impersonal commandments, objective laws, or universal formulas. The conditions for the events are the same as well: freedom, spontaneity, subjectivity, mutuality, and openness to the future. The event of encounter is a call for the novelty of a new relationship. And in the immediacy of that event truth is made. It is irrelevant to speak of "essences" in regard to the participants; it is because the participants are "unfinished" that relational immediacy can occur. What is essential is the connective "and"—the " 'and' within truth itself."[86] When Rosenzweig declares that what God reveals in revelation is "nothing but Himself to man," and when he asserts that "there is no 'essence of Judaism,' there is only: 'Hear O Israel!' "[87] there is reason to hope for transformative, dialogic exchange.

But it is the primary word "and" that is lost in Rosenzweig's description of Jewish-Christian relations (and of Jewish-non-Jewish relations in general); the "yes" and the "no" are voiced loudly, but without the relational "and," their sound is hollow. When Rosenzweig removes Judaism to a metaphysical plane, he takes it away from all connective experience and away from life itself. Moreover, the very divine-human relationship that he had intended to perfect is entirely distorted when Judaism becomes an atemporal fact. Had Rosenzweig maintained his emphasis on relational immediacy, he would have had to relinquish the notion of the eternality of the Jewish people. But he would have been able to sustain the insights of his New Thinking and thus the openness of Judaism to truth which might unfold in dialogue with representatives of other religions.

5

Martin Buber: Serving
Separately and Yet All Together

One of Martin Buber's most vivid memories was the scene which opened each class session of his early school years. Except for a small Jewish contingent, the majority of students at the Franz Joseph Gymnasium were Polish Catholics. "Personally the pupils got on well with one another, but the two groups as such knew almost nothing about each other." In general the "atmosphere" was one of "mutual tolerance without mutual understanding." At eight o'clock each morning, the class focused its attention on the large crucifix before which the teacher's desk was centered.

> . . . all the pupils stood up in their benches. The teacher and the Polish students crossed themselves; he spoke the Trinity formula, and they prayed aloud together. Until one might sit down again, we Jews stood silent and unmoving, our silent eyes glued to the floor.[1]

Beneath the "mutual tolerance" that allowed Jewish youths to study side-by-side with Polish youths was a thorough insensitivity to the differences which separated Christians and Jews. Precisely because the disrespect entailed in this classroom routine was not direct but rather impersonal, even unintended, the impact it had on Buber exceeded that of any outright abuse. For while the physical existence of the Jewish students was tolerated, their real presence, their personal existence, was not acknowledged.

> Compulsory guests, having to participate as a thing in a sacral event in which no dram of my person could or would take part, and this for eight long years morning after morning: that stamped itself upon the life-substance of the boy.[2]

The elements of this formative experience are repercussive throughout Buber's writings. Two related themes rebound time and again: First, what it means to be a person is to be a subject and to meet others as subjects, and second, what it means to know the truth is to stand in a relationship with another subject; truth is relational, not simply discovered but also established in relationship. These assertions are fundamental to Buber's understanding of

73

interhuman and interreligious dialogue. From the first flows respect for the individual; from the second, appreciation for traditions other than one's own.

For Buber, the purpose and the possibilities of human exchange can go well beyond that of mere tolerance for the individual or the tradition. Indeed, Buber asserts, "Our task is not to tolerate each other's waywardness but to acknowledge the real relationship in which both [Judaism and Christianity] stand to the truth."[3] That superbly concise statement is the core of Buber's position on the relationship between traditions and in particular on the relations between Judaism and Christianity.

Like Baeck and Rosenzweig, Buber works to engage Judaism in the modern world, speaking in such a way that the past vibrates sympathetically within the present. And like Rosenzweig, with whom Buber was closely associated, his method is dialogue.

> Hearkening to the human voice, where it speaks forth unfalsified, and replying to it, this above all is needed today. . . . This voice must not only be listened to, it must be answered and led out of the lonely monologue into the awakening dialogue of the peoples. Peoples must engage in talk with one another through their truly human men if the great peace is to appear and the devastated life of the earth renew itself.[4]

It is "fulfilled speech," speech which consists as much of sincere listening as of genuine speaking, upon which human salvation depends. Such speech is transformative; it takes us beyond an understanding of our differences and beyond the recognition of our commonalities to something "wholly different," which, Buber repeatedly admonishes, is as yet unknown and inexpressible — "a path [which] becomes visible where none suspected it."[5]

Buber stands apart from Baeck and Rosenzweig in his recognition of Christianity as a separate, valid, and valuable religion and in his belief that Christianity and Judaism are mutually important. This is not to say that he finds no fault with Christianity, especially Pauline Christianity, of which he has been accused of being hypercritical.[6] What Buber acknowledges is that Christianity has a place of its own; Christianity as it is interpreted by Paul and his followers essentially differs from Judaism, despite its rootage in it. (The Christianity of Jesus, on the other hand, is not distinguishable in any useful way from Judaism). Moreover, Buber argues that what Pauline Christianity has to say is of critical importance to Judaism and to the whole of humanity, just as what Judaism has to say is critically important to Christianity and to the whole of humanity. In genuine conversation with each other, the two traditions (and humanity in general) will be transformed by one another and thereby the image of the "great peace" will become more vivid.

With Buber, dialogue reaches a new level of power, surpassing that assigned to it by either Baeck or Rosenzweig. In asserting the need for both real speakers and real listeners in interfaith exchange, Buber envisions a dialogue whose goal reaches beyond tolerance, beyond understanding, and towards mutual and transformative advance.

Dialogue: "The Philosophy of the Interhuman"

For Buber, dialogue is an "ontic" category: its power is the power of creation. Not simply an instrument of creation, it is descriptive of the creative process as such. Something "happens" in dialogue, something spontaneous, novel, and more than the sum of its parts. In this "cradle of actual life,"[7] the basic word, I-You, is born and the relationality that underlies all reality is given a new mode of expression. In dialogue, one life takes shape in conscious response to another life, or more precisely, the one and the other become in response to each other's presence. "I require a You to become; becoming I, I say You."[8] In the creativity that is the dialogic process, the humanity of the human individual unfolds. And in the genuine relation of one individual to another, reality grows and truth is expanded.

To regard the encounter between two people as a psychological phenomenon alone is not to understand the event of encounter. In a psychological interpretation, the event is located either "in" the person or happens "to" the person;[9] our attention is directed either to the affected individual or to the effecting individual. In arguing against the dualism and reductionism inherent in such an interpretation, Buber proposes a third way of understanding human relations. The preposition proper to this way is "between"; it is between one being and another that personal existence comes to be. The "sphere of the between" is the "sphere of the interhuman,"[10] a dimension that is neither simply physical nor simply psychical, but, instead, is dialogical. Buber describes it as the place "where the souls end and the world has not yet begun."[11] When one individual embraces another, there arises a new reality that transcends the private world of each.

What happens in genuine encounter cannot be neatly divided into inner and outer events, into the assertion of one and the acceptance of the other, or even into a temporal first act and second act. The moment of meeting is a "two-fold movement" in which, however, "the primal setting at a distance," and the "entering into relation" are not temporally distinguishable.

> "First" and "second" are not to be taken in the sense of a temporal succession; it is not possible to think of an existence over against a world which is not also an attitude of relation. . . . one cannot stand in a relation to something that is not perceived as contrasted and existing for itself.[12]

It is only the human individual who is able to distinguish the self from the nonself, who is able to recognize that there is another reality, an "independent opposite" called not "I," but "world" or "other." The ability to see personal existence as set apart from other existences is distinctly human. But the ability to fill the distance with a new unity of presences, to negate the distance through mutual relation, is the "realization" of human life. "Distance provides the human situation; relation provides man's becoming in that situation."[13] Distance and relation are the poles of the process which is dialogue. What happens between them is human life.

Distance and relation is only one way, the more abstract way, of describing the dialectic of movement that is uniquely human. Buber also describes it as the act of seeking "confirmation" for one's existence from one's fellow human being. What does it mean to be confirmed? Above all it means "acceptance of otherness": this is at the root of what it means both *to* confirm and *to be* confirmed. For in recognizing the other, one sees oneself as distinct and in that distinctness one comes to terms with a wholeness that is uniquely one's own. That there are independent, nonidentical units which possess a wholeness that is not yet a unity is the "first movement of human life," the basis of "mutual existence."[14] From this presupposition the second movement, "mutual relation," is driven. The urge here is for a unity that is not mere compilation or assimilation, nor simply negation. Having sounded the "I" and heard a "you" echoing in the distance (but without the temporal lapse to distinguish call from reply), the becoming person forms the basic word, *I-Thou.* In so doing, the individual enters the world of relation, the world of actual life. The individual-in-relation participates in an actuality "that is neither merely a part of him nor merely outside him."[15] In the unity that arises from mutuality, the fullness of the other is confirmed in its elemental otherness by each partner.

The paradox of this affirmation of otherness is that the individual *feels* this otherness as if it were his or her own. Buber names this level of awareness "personal making present" and it hinges on the individual's ability to " 'imagine' the real."

> . . . 'imagining' the real means that I imagine to myself what another man is at this very moment wishing, feeling, perceiving, thinking, and not as a detached content but in his very reality, that is, as a living process in this man. The full 'making present' surpasses this in one decisive way: something of the character of what is imagined is joined to the act of imagining. . . .[16]

Sympathetic feeling, in the nontrivial sense, is offered as illustration:

> . . . that event in which I experience . . . the specific pain of another in such a way that I feel what is specific in it, not, therefore, a general discomfort or state of suffering, but this particular pain as the pain of the other.[17]

In confirming the other as an "I" for him or herself—as real and particular a human being as myself—I am presented with a "Thou" for me; and in relation with this "Thou," my own selfhood is affirmed.

It is important to repeat that this movement of "making present" is an ontological, rather than a psychological event. It is the fulfillment of the ontic category of relation. The thrust of Buber's argument and the point at which he differs so radically from modern personality theorists (and the advocacy of individualism in general) is that reality is *social*. The ontogenesis of the human individual is in accordance with this principle. Human beings are not self-sufficient but are dependent upon relationships of mutuality in order to grow as humans. Such relationships are ontologically complete only when "the other knows that he is made present by me in his self and when this knowledge induces the process of his inmost self-becoming."[18]

Language, in both its verbal and nonverbal forms, reflects and reinforces the social nature of humankind and of reality itself. It too has as its basic presupposition the acceptance of otherness. The words that well up at a distance, "in" an individual who exists apart from another, do not constitute real language. Indeed, monologue is the antithesis of fully valid speech; it is rather mere "speechifying." Here the actor is a performer, speaking to a "fictitious court of appeal,"[19] unaware of the realness and definiteness of the person who listens.

The monologue grounds nothing; it merely reflects. What is reflected is the speaker's self-impression; the listener is a mirror. Monologue tries to pass as a debate, a conversation, a friendly chat, a lovers' talk, but it lacks the mutuality present in genuine human exchange. The one who speaks into the mirror has no wish to communicate or learn something, no desire to influence or to relate to someone. The speechifier believes in the absoluteness of his or her position—all else is illegitimate, relativized, or questionable—and is happy to bask in the reflection of his or her "own glorious soul."[20] Buber calls monologue, in all its various disguises, a "conjuring force" of disintegration.[21] It never enters the realm of the between where individuals expose themselves and regard one another as they really are. It is only in the realm of the between that meaning "happens" and that interhuman truth is communicated.[22] In monologue neither of the basic words—*I-It* or *I-Thou*—are spoken; neither the "world as experience" nor the "world of relation" is meant. The vibrations of life—between association and detachment—are lost. The only movement is of the ego rocking itself into inactuality.[23]

Monologue is life-destroying because it does not recognize otherness. The meaning of otherness extends beyond the recognition that there are unique individuals who exist apart from me; Buber also uses it to mean *novelty*. What monologue lacks, in concrete terms, is "the moment of surprise."

The human person is not in his own mind unpredictable to himself as he is to any one of his partners: therefore, he cannot be a genuine partner to himself, he can be no real questioner and no real answerer.[24]

Dialogue is spontaneous and unpredictable — alive — because it is the meeting of (at least) two "present-making" individuals. Its outcome cannot be known in advance; finally, one does not know what one's response will be to the other's presence. "[A]n ordered world is not the world order." Dialogue is the "coming-to-be" of the person and the creation of a new occasion. The open-endedness of the future is complemented by the open-mindedness of the participants. Each must regard the other as both "for itself" and "for another," as both influencing and influenced. In relation, no one is purely passive or purely active. There is no other meaning of relation than reciprocity.[25]

To be open to another in this way means, paradoxically, that one has been seized by "the power of exclusiveness." What had been an "It" becomes transformed into that which is unique and immediate, into a particular and actual "Thou." The confirmation of another human being as this one and no other — not an exemplification of a type, not a part of a greater whole, not a product of objective analysis — this bold exclusiveness is what makes it possible for people to "act, help, heal, educate, raise, redeem."[26] Real partners act with the sort of concern that breaks through the barriers of the self. Buber contrasts such concern with Heidegger's notion in which, Buber contends, what is made accessible to the other is one's assistance but not one's self.[27] Such an occasion is no real relation since one person remains essentially unchanged, having offered only "solicitous help" and not the self per se.

Although the boundaries of the self are exploded in the realm of the between, the otherness or "over-againstness" of the two partners in a relationship is not dissipated. The uniqueness of the other is a necessary starting point for relationship *and* it is an essential affirmation throughout a genuine encounter. The desire to influence the other is not therefore lessened in fulfilled conversation. It does, however, take a different form than it might were the otherness of one's partner not confirmed. The desire to "inject one's own 'rightness'" into the other through coercive, propagandistic, or hypnotic means is destructive of real relationship. Here the other's personhood is denied; one encounters instead a "thing" which is to be externally pressured. In a genuine meeting, one partner may be the efficient cause for the change that occurs in the other, but one can never be the final cause. To influence one's partner means "to let that which is recognized as right, as just, as true (and for that very reason must also be established there, in the substance of the other) through one's influence take seed and grow in the form suited to individuation." Buber continues:

Men need, and it is granted to them, to confirm one another in their individual being by means of genuine meetings. But beyond this they need, and it is granted to them, to see the truth, which the soul gains by its struggle, light up to the others, the brothers, in *a different way, and even so be confirmed*.[28]

Dialogue that is genuine begins with the differences that separate and works to illuminate them so that a new and higher level of understanding might be reached. Buber calls dialogue's yield "a fruitfulness,"[29] and contrasts this with efforts to reach a common ground by assimilating, obscuring, or ignoring real differences. To reach this level, old differences are overcome in the "living towards the other" and become components of an ever-becoming, ever-new unity. From these roots grows a new life that is richer than its predecessor. And because the individual character of each person is never lost, this "fruitfulness" contains within it the seeds of future dialogue.

In the dialogical meeting, persons are created, "becoming I by saying Thou." Truth, too, comes to be in the relationship of the I to the Thou.

Whatever the meaning of the word "truth" may be in other realms, in the interhuman realm it means that men communicate themselves to one another as what they are.[30]

Truth that is reflective of the ontological process arises within the I-Thou relationship. It is what happens when persons respond authentically to one another. Truth, Buber contends, is not best described as a correspondence between appearance and reality or between the content of a proposition and its referent, but rather as an existential relationship, the I-Thou relationship.

Buber's vision of reality as the ever-arising relations between an I and a Thou, and not fundamentally as a dualism between subjects and objects, has been acclaimed as "the Copernican revolution" of modern thought.[31] Buber argues against the position that all knowledge is predicated on the external world. Rather, he contends, we arrive at an understanding of the world *after* we have established social relations with other persons. The I-Thou relationship precedes the I-It — the subject-object relationship — and not vice versa. We know the world of relations in an unmediated way, through encounter; the world of objects we know only as mediated through processes of intellection. What we know about ourselves, God, and the world, we know only through the engagement of a Thou-saying I with another Thou-saying I.

Knowledge of a reality shaped by the primacy of the I-Thou relationship is acquired in a way that is hostile to the scientific method. Indeed, it is no method at all, for real meeting — the arena of knowledge and meaning — cannot be premeditated or predicted. "The You encounters me by grace — it cannot be found by seeking."[32] Reality in its fullness will not reveal itself to one who is disengaged, who in looking "at" the world, looks away from her or himself. The world assumed by such a method is static, objective, and wholly external. It does not "open up" to the observer because the observer does not believe there is something inside to be opened up. If one approaches a potential "Thou" as an "It," only its "itness" will be revealed. And while all "Thou's" may become "It's" (and vice versa), to know reality in its "itness" is to know only a fragment of it, and to know it only as fragmented. But reality, for Buber, is not essentially disjointed, split between knowing subject and "known" objects. It is essentially a "union" of "Thou's," of personal presences committing themselves to other personal presences. Knowledge of this ultimate aspect of reality requires that one escape neither one's self nor the selfhood of the other, that one immerse oneself in the situation of relationship, and that one correlate one's own life with the life it meets in the great "between."

> To know signifies for the creature to fulfill a relation with being, for everyone in his own particular way, sincerely and with complete responsibility, accepting it on faith in all its various manifestations and therefore open to its real possibilities, integrating these experiences according to its nature. It is only in this way that the living truth emerges and can be preserved.[33]

"Objective truth," truth that is the product of the scientific method, is at best a partial description of reality and at worst a distortion of the full truth. When it is understood to be an inadequate but necessary expression of "relational truth" — truth that happens in dialogue between an I and a Thou — objective truth serves its purpose well. It forms the "chrysalis" for relational truth, giving it public form and temporal endurance. The processes of classification and systematization provide a content or "whatness" for relational truth. But the truth that happens in relationship between two persons cannot be summed up, calculated, or analyzed because it is not some "thing." The relation between an I and a Thou is an event which is neither temporally nor verbally repeatable. Exactly what happens in the moment of making-present cannot be articulated. And yet the effort must be made, preordained though it is to failure.

> All response binds the you into the It-world. That is the melancholy of man, and that is his greatness. For thus knowledge, thus works, thus image and example come into being among the living.[34]

Unlike Kierkegaard's knight of faith who is unable to convey anything about the revelatory experience to an outsider, the I-Thou event can be translated into I-It language and thereby become the inheritance of the next generation. It must be emphasized, however, that the legacy that is received is an imperfect, indeed crude sketch of the meeting itself. When the It-world knows its truth to be derivative from relational truth, when it recognizes that the expression it gives to intuition is inadequate, a complementary relationship exists between objective truth and relational truth. When, however, the It-world forgets that its objective truth points to something beyond itself, to something richer, more unified, and yet unfinished — and substitutes its half-knowledge for the whole, then science becomes scientism and there is conflict between the two realms.

Although the dialogical event cannot be structured by language, nonetheless something is said therein — an address is made and so is a response — and it is "said unto my very life,"[35] but no information or objective content is given. In the dialogical confrontation, the abstract other becomes a particular one who is known, however, without recourse to the particular attributes which serve as predicates for our subject-object language. What becomes known in dialogue is not "this" or "that" about the other. What becomes known is the other's *presence*. "Man receives, and what he receives is not a 'content' but a presence, a presence as strength."[36]

What has been said here of the encounter between human individuals also holds true with respect to the encounter between the individual and God. The divine-human dialogue is not essentially different from that which takes place between two human individuals. Rather, it is the exemplar of the I-Thou relationship. "I-Thou finds its highest intensity and transfiguration in religious reality, in which unlimited Being becomes, as absolute person, my partner."[37] God is the eternal Thou who by nature cannot become an It and this eternal Thou is met in every real meeting — "as soon as we touch a You, we are touched by a breath of eternal life." Reciprocity, confirmation of meaning, and verification in life are the three elements which characterize the meeting between two human beings and likewise the meeting between a human being and God. In addition, what becomes known in the moment of revelation, like that which becomes known in all I-Thou meetings, cannot be sufficiently expressed in language and may be properly responded to only in deed. "As we have nothing but a You on our lips when we enter the encounter, it is with this on our lips that we are released from it into the world." In divine revelation, God is not named except as "I am there as whoever I am there"[38] and God's message to the individual is not recountable in words.

Buber's understanding of truth as a relational event which lacks content (in the usual, transmissable form) has important ramifications for the encounter between traditions. It is clear from what has been said before about the dialogical moment that one's attitude toward oneself and toward the other is of utmost importance. For creative communion to occur, the participants must approach the situation with commitment and with openness, asserting their selfhood and yet living toward the other, aware of the unfinished nature of their lives and alive to the adventure of forming a new unity. But beyond this, the whole activity of dialogue takes on an enormous importance insofar as dialogue gives rise to truth. For Buber, the aim of religion is to center the life of humanity on the presence of God. And the making-present of God takes place not in isolation from one's neighbors, but in direct and conscious turning toward them. "Above and below are bound to one another. The word of him who wishes to speak with men without speaking with God is not fulfilled; but the word of him who wishes to speak with God without speaking with men goes astray."[39] The message that is given in dialogue with God, in revelation, is clarified in dialogue with other human beings. The activity of turning to one another in dialogue which issues in the creation and communication of truth is not something to be left to the occasional ecumenical impulse. Rather, it should be the decisive activity in which members of a religious tradition engage.

Furthermore, the claims that can be made about one's tradition are restricted in accordance with the parameters Buber sets for dialogical truth. What is revealed in the encounter is revealed as an address to the particular individual, not as a universally valid, eternally inscribed dictum. The message is tied to the situation in which it is delivered and received and therefore cannot be lifted out of its context without a dissipation of its meaning and its power. For Buber, then, claims of absolutism and exclusivity are antithetical to reality and the revelation by which reality is communicated. In comparing himself to Luther and Calvin who made just such claims, Buber writes:

> . . . the word of God crosses my vision like a falling star to whose fire the meteorite will bear witness without making it light up for me, and *I myself can only bear witness to the light but not produce the stone and say, "This is it."*[40]

Traditions that attempt to secure their revelations by filling them with content — with religious dogma and moral principles meant to endure forever — construct a graveyard instead. The present is buried in a past "once-for-all," the moment of revelation is no longer the catalyst for new individuals, new unities, new truths, or new realities. "Dogma, even when its claim of origin remains uncontested, has become the most exalted form of invulnerability against revelation. Revelation will tolerate no perfect tense."[41] Past revelations must give way to the present moment and the novel revelation it yields. Indeed, the past gives way by becoming something new. "Memory itself is changed as it plunges from particularity into wholeness."[42]

In turning now from theory to practice, from a discussion of Buber's dialogical method to an application of the method of dialogue to the Jewish — Christian encounter, Buber's primary insight might again be stated:

> We are created along with one another and directed to a life with one another. Creatures are placed in my way so that I, their fellow creature, by means of them and with them find the way to God. A God reached by their exclusion would not be the God of all lives in whom all life is fulfilled. . . . God wants us to come to him by means of the Reginas he has created and not by renunciation of them.[43]

On Judaism

In 1909, at the request of a group of young Jewish students, Buber delivered three lectures in which he addressed the question plaguing the Jewish intelligentsia of the time: "Why do we call ourselves Jews? . . . What does it mean for us to want perpetuity, not merely as human beings . . . but in defiance of both Time and this particular time, as Jews?"[44] Buber's impact on his audience was profound. In the words of one of his listeners, the answers Buber offered "brought hope into the hearts of European Jewry of the year 1909 . . . and utterly changed the spiritual course of Jewish youth in Central Europe."[45]

Buber's approach was both descriptive, focusing on the notion of Jewish "religiosity," and programmatic, calling for the "renewal of Judaism." The two aspects, however, were not separable: "Renewal of Judaism means in reality renewal of Jewish religiosity." For Buber, the essential character of Judaism, the basis for its uniqueness, and the reason for its continuation, is its embodiment of genuine "religiosity." The term "religiosity" includes a number of related characteristics, but primarily it refers to an "elemental God-consciousness," to the "elemental entering-into-relation with the absolute."[46] The I-Thou relationship between an individual and God, or in the case of Judaism, between a people and God, is what constitutes, for Buber, the basis of concrete religious life.

In naming the I-Thou relationship as the essence of religiosity, and of Jewish religiosity in particular, Buber distinguishes himself in two ways from the discussion about Judaism that was then current. First, he differs from those who, in their efforts to find a place for Judaism in the modern world, argued that it is primarily either an ethical system, a religious creed, or a national movement. According to Buber, Judaism *includes* these elements, but they do not constitute its definitive structure. Such attempts to fit Judaism into a category that would be recognized by the non-Jewish world as "religion" make an abstraction out of that which is a concrete totality: a way of life. "In the last resort, 'religious life' means concreteness itself, the whole concreteness of life *without reduction*, grasped dialogically, included in the dialogue."[47] Neither ethical monotheism nor political Zionism captured the unique character of Judaism. Buber was even more emphatic about the inability of Orthodox Judaism — even as qualified by Samson Raphael Hirsch — to express the spirit of Judaism because Orthodoxy confines Judaism to what has been handed-down, passively accepted, and narrowly defined. It is here that Buber distinguishes himself again from the usual form of then current discussions of Judaism. He asserts that a difference must be drawn between "religiosity" and "religion," and that this difference is as great as the difference between creativity and repetition, between presence and memory. Religion is derivative of religiosity; it is the "sum total of the customs and teachings articulated and formulated by the religiosity of a certain epoch in a people's life." In its positive

light, religion is the "organizing" principle for the creativity which bursts forth
from the religious encounter with God. Too often, however, religion asserts its
independence from the creative principle, declares itself to be the true medium
for revelation, and formalizes the message into dogma and law: When that
occurs, meaning and truth depart from religion and it becomes a "rubble"
from which Jewish religiosity must be extricated.

> Religion is true so long as it is creative; but it is creative only so long as
> religiosity, accepting the yoke of the laws and doctrines, is able . . . to imbue
> them with new and incandescent meaning, so that they will seem to have been
> revealed to every generation anew, revealed today, thus answering men's very
> own needs, needs alien to their fathers.[48]

What Buber means by "religiosity" can be summed up in the Hebrew word,
emunah, "trust, resulting from an original relationship to the Godhead," in
which the "immediacy of the whole man is directed towards the whole God."[49]
And according to Buber, the best exemplification of religiosity — both Jewish
and non-Jewish — is to be found in the community of the Hasidim. Actualizing
the spirit of *emunah*, this community is the incarnation of true or "absolute"
Judaism, of Judaism that does not mold itself to the world, but which works to
mold the world after its image of the Kingdom of God. The "innate tendencies"[50] of the Jewish spirit which become encrusted in "religion" are lived out in
the religiosity of the Hasid.

There are three "innate tendencies" and they revolve around two foci. The
first focus of the Jewish soul is the immediate, relational presence of God; the
second is the redemptive power of God at work in an as yet unredeemed
world. Here is the I-Thou relationship in its religious translation. The Jewish
response to these fundamental experiences is triadic, paralleling the three
processes of creation, revelation, and redemption. The "innate tendencies,"
like the processes to which they correspond, are distinguishable but not separable. They are the ideas of *unity, deed,* and *the future*. The drive toward unity,
the "primal process within," presupposes the other two basic ideas, for it
requires active, outward movement or deed, and it finds its final perfection in
the idea of a messianic future. Together, unity, deed, and the future constitute
the Jewish soul, which throughout the generations has remained unchanged
(although those who possessed such a soul were often not true to it). Buber
stresses that these ideas are not mere abstractions, but are formative of Jewish
existence.

> I mean innate predispositions of a people's ethos that manifest themselves with
> such great force and so enduringly that they produce a complex of spiritual
> deeds and values which can be called the people's absolute life.[51]

The innate predisposition of the Jewish people is to be peculiarly sensitive to the "dualism," or absence of wholeness that pervades human life. For other people, the sense of disunity is vague, indirect, or subordinate; for the Jew it is "inordinate," "central," pure, and full. Judaism answers this overwhelming sense of inner duality with *emunah*, with trust in the presence of God working to redeem the world. In Judaism's recognition of this primal dualism, in its efforts to overcome it by performing deeds through which God can be realized, and in its vision of a future, unified world, Judaism surpasses every other religious tradition. In having found an answer to its intense experience of duality, Judaism establishes its role for humanity: it is the messenger and model of the life of dialogue and thereby of unity.

> This, then, is, and continues to be, Judaism's fundamental significance for mankind: that, conscious as is no other community of the primal dualism, knowing and typifying division more than any other community, it proclaims a world in which dualism is abolished, a world of God which needs to be realized in both the life of individual man and the life of the community: the world of unity.[52]

The matrix in which unity comes to be is life-in-community, and the prototype for such a community is the way of the Hasidim. Here the consciousness of God is especially vivid, and hence the overcoming of dualism is especially effective. Here the spirit of religiosity is unencumbered by dogma or ritual, and individuals are urged to seek out God for themselves in their own ways. Quoting the Baal Shem, Buber writes:

> We say "God of Abraham, God of Isaac and God of Jacob": we do not say "God of Abraham, Isaac and Jacob," so that you may be told: Isaac and Jacob did not rely on Abraham's tradition, but they themselves searched for the Divine.[53]

Here the dialogue with God turns to a dialogue with one's neighbors, with nature, and with the whole of humanity, and these dialogues turn again toward God. God's immanence provides the basis of the hallowing of all life so that there is no split between the sacred and profane and between religious deed and everyday activity. Meaning is granted to concrete life, which in turn makes present God's redemptive powers. In this community, then, in life shared with others, the messianic future is made ever more present.

To the question, Is there an inherently Jewish religiosity? Buber gives a resounding "yes." The basis for this affirmative reply is his belief that there is a "unique relationship to the unconditioned which can be called essentially Jewish."[54] Buber does not, however, mean that the kind of relationship a Jew has with God is unparalleled by any other religious tradition. He means rather that the relationship between Jews and God has an intensity not attained by other peoples.

> I am far from wishing to contend that the conception and the experience of the dialogical situation are confined to Judaism. But I am certain that no other community of human beings has entered with such strength and fervor into this experience as have the Jews.[55]

The difference is one of degree, not of kind. It is the difference between the relationship of an *individual* and the relationship of a *people*—a society of individuals—with God.

According to Buber, the Sinai event is unique not because here, for the first time, God encountered these people, but because here God and Israel established a *new* relationship, corresponding to an essentially new situation. At Sinai a group of individuals gathered who recognized themselves as a national-political entity, as a people. During the time spent overcoming the Egypt years, the divisiveness of tribal relations slowly gave way to a new consciousness of unity. The situation which leads to the covenant at Sinai is defined by this new consciousness of peoplehood. God "makes known His will first of all as constitution—not constitution of cult and custom only, also of economy and society."[56] It is a covenant between God and a *people* with national and political concerns who, at Sinai, commits itself to placing these concerns within a theological framework. The covenant, as Buber understands it, is a "religio-political, a theo-political, act."[57]

This covenant welds religion and politics, creed and nation, into a single unit whose actual form is the people of Israel. Ordinary life is no longer ordinary; it is the place in which religious ideals become reality. "The theism of Israel is characterized finally in this, that the faith-relations according to its nature wishes to be valid for and to bear upon all life."[58] This is most possible when it is a whole people which enters the faith-relation rather than a single individual. Thus Buber's belief in the necessity of community life for religious experience *and* his belief that the hyphenated nature of Judaism—its theo-political structure—makes it the exemplary representative of the I-Thou relationship. Peoplehood is the source of Israel's uniqueness and of Israel's vocation among the nations.

The covenant is a summons to live in and as a faith-community in response to God's presence in the world, and to build the messianic kingdom by calling upon the nations to live in this manner. "Israel's function is to encourage the nations to change their inner structures"—structures which promote the primal dualism by separating the political from the religious realms, the world "below" from the world "above," and the actual world from the ideal world—"and their relations to one another."[59] As the first *people* to respond to God as the "ardently singular Thou"[60] who is involved in the totality of life, and thus as the "first real attempt at 'community,'" the Jewish people is empowered to enter world history as a "prototype" of engagement in life with God.[61] "[I]t exists as a people only because 'peoplehood' is the presupposition of the *whole* human response to God. . . . The community must endure as a presupposition of the fulfillment."[62] The world is as yet unredeemed, but redemption comes, is coming, through life in community.

The Jewish people is not always loyal to its vocation, and the generation that Buber addresses is, according to him, especially errant. It is something other than, something less than, a community-in-the-presence-of-God. The "inner reality" of Judaism has been distorted by two conflicting forces, that of tradition and that of assimilation (called, respectively, by Buber, "Jewish inertia" and "Judaism as a 'humanitarianism' "). And yet despite the inauthenticity of its external existence, this generation harbors within it the "soul" of Judaism, the absolute life for which it is meant. Its appearance belies its reality for the spirit of Judaism cannot depart from the Jewish people who once received a task as a people. "[H]aving, through this summons, become a people, it inviolably preserved its knowledge, despite all its own defects, weaknesses, and failures."[63] It is on the basis of biological inheritance that Buber argues for the continuing uniqueness of Judaism and its mission to the world despite the post-Enlightenment decline in Jewish communal life.

Every Jew, no matter how assimilated or secularized, may find within the deep structures of his or her self a "substance" or "blood" which is definitive of the person he or she is. "My soul is not by the side of my people; my people *is* my soul." The biological relationship of the present individual with the people — past, present, and future — gives the Jew an innate disposition or "form" according to which the external environment is assimilated. That historical revelation in which the Jews identified themselves and were recognized to be a people — the basis of Jewish unity, uniqueness, and significance — is transmitted biologically. The Jew is an Oriental and as such, Buber writes:

> He has preserved within himself the limitless motor faculties that are inherent in his nature, and their attendant phenomena, a dominant sense of time and a capacity for quick conceptualization. He has also preserved within himself, sometimes buried but never completely crushed, *his elemental unitary drive and the motif of demand.* One can detect all this in the most assimilated Jew, if one knows how to gain access to his soul; and even those who have eradicated the last vestiges of Judaism from the content of their thinking still, and ineradicably, carry Judaism with them in the pattern of their thought.[64]

The idea of a "racial memory" at work in Buber's conception of Judaism makes possible his claim for the intensity of feelings, both of unity and disunity, that are felt by all Jews.[65]

In summary, the goal that Buber sets before his young audience is to renew themselves as Jews by returning to genuine Jewish religiosity — to a life lived in community with others and in dialogue with God.

The Relationship between Judaism and Christianity

Buber has been reproached for being excessively critical and one-sided in his evaluation of Christianity.[66] When he speaks of Judaism, he mixes the actual with the possible, overlaying historical realities with the ideal. When discussing Christianity, however, Buber's approach is primarily descriptive: he considers neither the ideal on which Christianity is based nor the ideal after which it strives. Moreover, in his descriptive analysis of Christianity, Buber often reduces the complexity of a rich historical tradition to a simplistic and exaggerated form. These tendencies to describe and simplify result in a construction of Christianity that is clearly inferior to his idealized Judaism. Yet despite all this, Buber maintains a high regard for Christianity, believing it to be both a fully legitimate way to God and a source of mystery that can enrich our understanding of Judaism and of reality in general.

In Buber's encounter with Christianity, there are several unresolved tensions which create the sense that earnest dialogue is in contention with immoderate criticism. These can be summarized broadly in two ways. The more general one is between Buber's recognition on the one hand that Christianity is, like Judaism, an "authentic sanctuary" whose "mystery" can be acknowledged but not judged (since what is not known from within cannot be judged) and on the other hand, Buber's description of what he understands Christianity to be and his evaluation of it. The second tension is rooted in the typology Buber uses to describe the two faiths—a typology which, on the one hand, shows Judaism to be superior and, on the other hand, shows Christianity to be a satisfactory way to salvation and, moreover, a way which may have something important to say to Judaism. What is disclosed, albeit imperfectly, in these tensions is Buber's commitment to the kind of dialogue which requires partners who are at once *over-against* one another and yet *open* to one another.

> We serve, separately and yet all together, not by each of us shirking his reality of belief nor by surreptitiously seeking a togetherness despite our difference, but rather when acknowledging our fundamental difference, we impart to each other in unreserved confidence what we know of the unity of this house.[67]

According to Buber, there are two, and only two, basic forms that religious faith takes, with Christianity and Judaism typifying the two. The Christian type of faith is characterized as *pistis*, as a "relationship of acknowledgment," based on the acceptance of a proposition about the object of faith. The Jewish type of faith is characterized as *emunah*, as a "relationship of trust," arising out of an immediate "contact" with the one in whom one trusts.[68] The two types have their origins within two different sociological settings: Christian faith occurs primarily in individuals who are not intimately related to a community, but who join together as a consequence of their conversions. Jewish faith, on the other hand, occurs in individuals who understand themselves to be members of a community. These people find themselves in a living relationship of trust, surrounded as they are by a community which has covenanted itself to the Unconditioned. To the faith of *pistis* one must be converted, exchanging an old way of thinking for a new way. In contrast, the faith of *emunah* is lived in continuity with the life of the community.

When Buber initially introduces these two types of faith, he does not intimate that there is a difference between the two, either in their degree of truth or in their existential value. They are presented as two ways of being, both of which engage the entire being of the individual in relationship with God and are not necessarily in conflict, reflecting as they do different existential situations as their points of origin. It is only as Buber elaborates on the content of these orientations that the differences become antitheses and the thesis that is Judaism appears to be the correct one.

At the outset, Buber declares his fraternity with Jesus. In Jesus' "impulses and stirrings,"[69] he is thoroughly Jewish; in his criticism of Jewish law and ritual, Jesus is a solid member of the Pharisaic community; in his encounter with God and his community, he actualizes the I-Thou relationship, based on *emunah*, to the fullest extent. Buber calls upon Jews to make a place for this "great brother"—a place which "cannot be described by any of the usual categories." Moreover, Buber responds with seriousness to the Christian claim that Jesus is God and Savior; it is a claim which, "for his sake and my own, I must endeavor to understand."[70]

But although Buber makes the important acknowledgment that Jesus cannot be placed within the "usual" categories of Jewish thought, he does not go so far as to place Jesus within a unique category. Instead, he regards Jesus as a "suffering servant of God," one of the generations of suffering servants. Thus Buber's understanding of Jesus is not revolutionary, and the seriousness with which he approaches the Christian claim of Jesus' divinity is difficult to gauge. Buber places Jesus within the category of existence whose essence is "hiddenness," unselfconsciousness, and absence of premeditation. It is as "concealed arrows in God's quiver" that these individuals serve the cause of redemption. The "messianic mystery" is that redemption is set in motion by those who remain within the quiver.

> Their hiddenness belongs to the essence of their work of suffering. Each of them can be the fulfilling one; none of them in his self-knowledge may be anything other than a servant of the Lord.[71]

The notion of hiddenness operates in several ways. On the personal level it is unselfconscious action; the deed is done not as an act of self but as an act of the self-in-relationship-with-God. And, because the redemptive need is panoramic, the individual's efforts to work in concert with God are also "hidden" though not lost. On the public or community level, hiddenness is the unannounced work that brings the Kingdom of God into those concrete forms that define the everyday, "hiding" the sacred within the profane world and thereby redeeming the world without unraveling it. Hiddenness is the means for continuity, both for the continuity of creation—there is no break between redeemed and unredeemed time—and for the continuity of personal responsibility. Where there is no saving knowledge, every act of the individual has bearing on the creative-redemptive process. The paradoxical nature of "hiddenness" is this: it is in concealment that the redemptive process reveals itself. The assertion that the Messiah has come is thus destructive of the messianic process. "Messianic self-disclosure is the bursting of Messiahship."[72]

Why "hiddenness" is essential to messianic action has its explanation in Buber's understanding of redemption and the redemptive process. Redemption and dialogue are one and the same process—the process of "bringing into relationship." The redemptive process thus has all the qualities of the dialogical relationship: mutuality, spontaneity, presentness, individuality, lack of finality, sanctification of the concrete life, and the inability of language to capture the essence of the event. Negatively described, neither dialogue nor the redemptive process is univocal, premeditated, temporally transcendent, general, final, abstract, or amenable to the articulations of dogma. For Buber, the declaration that one person is the Messiah is also the declaration that the dialogical relationship has been superceded. For in its absoluteness, the Messiah makes unnecessary the responsiveness required in a life based on mutuality. Finality destroys mutuality, novelty, and human "response-ability." Concrete, actual life is trivialized and human action is emptied of power and meaning. The gift of the Messiah is confidence and security, purchased, however, at the price of life itself. The security of salvation that is disclosed in a proclamation of messiahship works against the actual process of redemption!

Security is the sign of the false messiah. In contrast, Buber offers the notion of "holy insecurity," of life lived with the trust that redemption is unrealized but ever-occurring. Redemption is not a once-and-for-all event whose locus is a single individual, but an "unbroken chain of meetings, each of which demands the person for what can be fulfilled by him, just by him and just in this hour."[73]

When Jesus steps out of the quiver (albeit in "highest innocence."[74]), he becomes the "first in the series" of false messiahs. The claim of messiahship—whether made self-consciously or imposed from without—is, according to Buber, "a mishap [which befalls] the reality between man and God."[75] It is a mishap of major proportions because it drives a wedge between the dialogical relationship of the I with the Thou. The "wedge" is the perfect person whose perfection erases all distinctions—between sacred and profane, good and evil, the world-that-is and the world-to-come, and finally between the human and divine — so that they appear in the hour of completion to have been merely provisional and temporary.

> Of this [perfected] man nothing more is demanded, he is free from all "ought"; for all that should be is here already done, man is as he is, he lives as he lives, and therein he has his perfection.[76]

Dialogue, as the process in which creation, revelation, and redemption occur, is no longer necessary.

But Buber distinguishes between the Jesus who steps from the shadow of servitude and becomes Christ to his followers and the Jesus who is the Jew from Nazareth. Jesus the Jew did not desire to know the mysteries of God but rather lived a life of *devotio*, of "unredeemed service . . . to the divine made present as over against me."[77] And he acted in the spirit of *emunah*, of trust, thus addressing God as "Father."[78] This is the man whom Buber claims to know, as all Jews do, "from within . . . in a way that remains inaccessible to the peoples submissive to him."[79] The way that Jesus followed and advocated, up until the messianic disclosure, was Jewish through and through, its "motive power" being the "ancient Jewish demand for the unconditioned decision, a decision that transforms man and lifts him into the divine realm."[80] In a world of distinctions, of "cruel contradictions," decision is the formative act of the individual. The decisive act which places one in active relationship with God is "the *quiet* work of overcoming the contradictions."[81] According to Buber, what Jesus taught and what "original" Judaism teaches are one and the same and this is why the Nazarene movement belongs "in the spiritual history of Judaism."[82]

But Buber goes beyond reclaiming early Christianity as a part of the prophetic tradition that undergirds Jewish spirituality. In his lectures on Judaism he asks his listeners:

> . . . may we not answer those who are currently recommending to us a "rap-prochement" with Christianity: "Whatever in Christianity is creative is not Christianity but Judaism; and this we need not reapproach; we need only to recognize it within ourselves and to take possession of it, for we carry it within us, never to be lost. But whatever in Christianity is not Judaism is uncreative, a mixture of a thousand rites and dogmas; with this — we say it both as Jews and as human beings — we do not want to establish a rapprochement."[83]

Here Buber repeats the assessment of Christianity given by Baeck and Rosenzweig: Christianity is not *essentially* different from Judaism, but is rather an unfortunate degeneration of the Jewish spirit by Hellenic influences. The "Christianity" of Jesus is "original" Judaism. In his understanding of the original, Jesus "outshines" the members of his community — the Pharisees — who also sought to exemplify it. From out of his eschatological perspective, Jesus brought the demands of Torah to a new level of intensity. "It is indeed always so when a person in the sign of the *Kairos* demands the impossible in such a way that he compels men to will the possible more strongly than before."[84] It is this Jesus, placed within his historical-biographical setting, whom Buber knows from within, as a member of the family.

It is not the intensity of Jesus' demands that separates Judaism from Christianity, but the claim of Jesus' messiahship. It is Paul who deifies Jesus and in so doing makes of him for the Jewish world the initiator of that series of people—ending with Shabbetai Zevi—who discloses the messianic secret and thus conceals its meaning. About this Jesus, Buber says:

> That this first one in the series was incomparably the purest, most rightful of them all, the one most endowed with real messianic power, does not alter the fact that he was the first, yea, it belongs rather to it, belongs to that awful and pathetic character of reality which clings to the whole messianic series.[85]

It is clear from this passage, that, in Buber's estimation, Jesus' entrance into the ranks of the automessianists was a serious loss for Judaism. It is not clear, however, that Buber also believes it to be a loss for the world at large, even though those who hold to the divinity of Jesus hold to an "awful" and "pathetic" sense of reality. He writes the following of Dostoevski's character in *The Possessed* who "falteringly has to confess that he indeed believes in Christ, but in God he will believe," and others who view their relationship with Christ as more immediate and more meaningful than their relationship with God:

> I see in all this an important testimony to the salvation which has come to the Gentiles through faith in Christ: they have found a God Who did not fail in times when their world collapsed, and further, One Who in times when they found themselves sunk under guilt granted atonement. This is something much greater than what an ancestral god or son of the gods would have been able to do for this late age. And something akin to that testimony resounds to us from the cries and groans of earlier generations to Christ.[86]

Buber recognizes that the relationship that Christians have with God through Christ is, like that of Jews with God, a relationship of immediacy. But it is a "new and different kind of immediacy," comparable to the immediacy one has with a "beloved person, who has just this and no other form and whom one has chosen precisely as this form." Through this concrete expression of personhood, the believer is moved to a level of intimacy which extends "to the merging of the self, to the self-bearing of this suffering, to the self-receiving of these wounds and wound marks and to a love for man which 'proceeds from Him.'" Buber affirms, then, the benefits of Christianity for those who adhere to it; and he also affirms the uniqueness of the relationship that the Christian has with God, and hence the uniqueness of Christianity as a "life relationship."[87]

But Buber's assessment of the value of Christianity for Christians is hardly extravagant. At the end of the paragraph quoted above, Buber states, "Only one must not miss hearing the other thing when listening to their [Christians'] fervor and piety." The "other thing" that we should hear is the Christian tendency toward "ditheism," the worship of the "Lord Jesus" instead of God. The Christian relationship to God is unlike the Jewish relationship precisely because its immediacy is with one whose face is seen. Jewish immediacy is built on the paradox that God's presence is revealed in God's invisibility. Revelation and concealment require each other in order that the imageless God not be hidden, that is, "fix[ed] to one manifestation," but remains present "as the One Who is there as He is there."[88] It is this paradox that is dissolved by the Christian form of immediacy. For although the imaged God is only one aspect of the Christian God who is also imageless (Christ as "the image of the invisible God," Col. 1:15), Buber argues that in the actual life of Christians, the imageless One is concealed by the imaged One.[89] Because of this concealment, the Christian relationship of immediacy is seriously threatened. The intimacy gained from meeting God in human form, the concreteness of Christianity, is gained at the expense of immediacy. And this is an unacceptable paradox for Buber.

In the remainder of his book on Judaism and Christianity (excluding the final chapter), Buber's argument for the overall inadequacy of the Christian model of relational immediacy and, in contrast, the adequacy of the Jewish model, is unfolded. Paul is described as having "contended for both things at once, for loyalty to the highest possible conception of his Master and for the 'unweakened' maintenance of monotheism," and finally, as having failed. His failure is, for Buber, the failure of all of Christianity. In chapters thirteen through sixteen, Buber builds on Augustine's observation that Paul "says very little about the love of men to God."[90] Buber contends that this is so because Paul is unable to hold together the *middot* or qualities which simultaneously constitute a part of God's nature.[91] No longer do God's anger and God's tenderness, God's wrath and God's reconciliation, God's judgment and God's grace, God's farness and God's nearness form unities within God. For Paul separates the *middot* and bestows the "negative" set of attributes on God — anger, judgment, absence — and the "positive" set of attributes on Christ — tenderness, grace, presence. Under these conditions, it is not humanity alone which requires a mediator, but God as well. As immediacy between Christ and humanity is established, that between God and humanity is "abolished." It is abolished in prayer and in every attempt by Paul to deal with the "contradictions of existence" such as human suffering, injustice, and isolation.

> There is for him [Paul] in the course of history no immediacy between God and
> man, but only at the beginning and end. . . . 'I am the door' it now runs (John
> 10:9); it avails nothing, as Jesus thought, to knock where one stands (before the
> 'narrow door'); it avails nothing as the Pharisees thought, to step into the open
> door; entrance is only for those who believe in 'the door.'[92]

It is Paul's relentless dualism that is responsible for the loss of immediacy
between the Christian and God. Whether there is another way to "contend
with both things"—with the imaged Christ and the imageless God—Buber
does not inquire. Indeed, he disregards the centuries of trinitarian and christo-
logical debates. The force of his argument is that Pauline Christianity fails to
maintain the level of immediacy between God and humanity attained by
Pharisaic or original Judaism. Immediacy, as the "primal reality of a life
relationship,"[93] is Buber's measure of the strength of the I-Thou relationship.
And it is in the imageless religion, in Judaism, that immediacy is most fully
embraced.

Elsewhere Buber poses his criticism of Christian immediacy in different
terms. In *The Origin and Meaning of Hasidism*, Buber links the emphasis on
nationhood in Hasidic thought to the Hasidic understanding of redemption.
In response to those who wonder why Hasidism didn't become "one of the
great religions of redemption in the world," Buber answers, "It could not pass
to humanity because it could not disconnect the redemption of the soul from
the redemption of the nation." It is this organic structure between the individual and his or her people, between the people and their nation, that Buber
holds to be the foundation for the vitality of the divine-human relationship and
thus for the redemption of the world.

> The action of Christianity at the time of her separation from Judaism, her
> forsaking of the idea of the holiness of the nation, and the absolute value of its
> task, could not be imitated by Hasidism, for, in the eyes of Hasidism, between
> the world and the individual there is an intermediate existence which cannot be
> overlooked—the nation.[94]

Buber recognizes no irony in his position that the nation is an "intermediate
existence" necessary to world redemption. For this intermediate existence,
unlike the Christian mediator, serves to heighten the efficacy and immediacy
of the divine-human encounter. When the individual is set apart and saved
apart from his or her community, the unity of redemption is broken and hence
the I-Thou relationship is weakened. Then "people became Christians only as
individuals, but the nations as nations remained idol worshippers."[95] This
indeed is the "crisis of Pistis" for modern Christians: the ever-widening "dis-
parity between the sanctification of the individual and the accepted unholi-
ness" of the community. The solution to this crisis is to seek a "form of Pistis

nearer to Emunah."[96] Since *emunah* presupposes membership in a community
which is conscious of itself as a people covenanted to God, Buber is advocating
a new form of Christianity, a more Jewish form.

In the last chapter of his book, *Two Types of Faith*, Buber returns to the initial
distinction he had drawn between Judaism and Christianity, between *emunah*
and *pistis*. "The faith of Judaism and the faith of Christianity are by nature
different in kind, each in conformity with its human basis." That distinction
implies a difference in origin — Judaism arose as a part of a national soul and
Christianity arose "outside the historical experiences of nations" and within the
"souls of individuals."[97] It does not necessarily imply that one religion is superior to the other in the relationship it fosters between the individual and God.
In the final analysis, however, this is Buber's position. Christianity is indeed
an "authentic sanctuary"[98] in which the I-Thou relationship is to be found. It is
not Christianity's authenticity that Buber challenges, however, but its efficacy.
In its reliance upon mediatorship and in its emphasis on the individual over
the community, Christianity deprives the I-Thou relationship of its most
intense form of immediacy.

Martin Buber's position on Jewish-Christian relations (and, by extension,
on interreligious relations as a whole) does not, however, close with an assertion about Judaism's superiority to Christianity (and, by implication, to other
religions). It ends instead with a reemphasis on the necessity of openness and
the essential activity of dialogue. Having defined the sort of "passionate"
position that readies one for dialogue, Buber moves ahead to consider the
difficult task of dialogue between individuals who are committed to their
positions and, in the case of Judaism and Christianity, whose positions are in
many ways mutually exclusive.

> We can try to do something extremely difficult, something which is extremely
> difficult for the religiously oriented person, something which runs counter to his
> orientation and relationships or, rather, seems to run counter to them, some-
> thing which seems to run counter to his relationship with God. We can acknowl-
> edge as a *mystery* that which, notwithstanding our existence and self-knowledge,
> others confess as their reality of belief.[99]

The great mystery at work in the universe is the mystery of unity forming
out of tremendous diversity. Part of this mystery is that two faiths can contradict one another and yet have something to say to each other that is true.
According to Buber, this is the paradox within which Jews and Christians live.
What Jews know about themselves and thereby about Christianity is "fundamentally and irreconcilably different" from what Christians know about themselves and thereby about Judaism.[100] Jews know that they have a relationship
of personal immediacy with a God who is imageless, a relationship which has
not been contravened. Christians know themselves to be the true Israel, to

have a relationship with God that supercedes Judaism's relationship, secured as it is by the incarnation of God in the Messiah. Whether God has been incarnated in the messianic figure of Jesus and whether the continuity of history has been broken by the messianic redemption — these form the human perspectives which are resolved for Buber only in the "mystery" that is finally God's truth.

It is not, however, sufficient merely to maintain a "common watch for a unity to come." Even though this unity "soar[s] above all of your imagination and all of ours," we must work to anticipate its form.[101] Buber ends his book on Jewish-Christian "interpenetration" with this important suggestion:

> . . . an Israel striving after the renewal of its faith through the rebirth of the person and a Christianity striving for the renewal of its faith through the rebirth of nations would have something as yet unsaid to say to each other and a help to give one another — hardly to be conceived at the present time.[102]

Here it is clear that Buber's conception of dialogue extends well beyond that of Baeck's and Rosenzweig's. Those who hold a firm position can yet remain "open to the world" and thereby grow "more and more true to reality" without also becoming less true to themselves.[103]

> It behooves both you and us to hold inviolably fast to our own true faith, that is to our deepest relationship to truth. It behooves both of us to show a religious respect for the true faith of the other. This is not what is called "tolerance," our task is not to tolerate each other's waywardness but *to acknowledge the real relationship in which both stand to the truth*. Whenever we both, Christian and Jew, care more for God himself than for our images of God, we are united in the feeling that our Father's house is differently constructed than our human models take it to be.[104]

Truth is approached through dialogue between partners who strive to "acknowledge the *real relationship* in which both [partners] stand to the truth," and who seek a mutual deepening of their imperfect imaginations and of their unfinished truths.

Critical Reassessment

Buber's approach to dialogue is grounded in his understanding of reality as fundamentally social or relational. From this basic affirmation, a number of notions follow which together constitute Buber's method of dialogue. These notions may be summarized as follows: 1) "Real meeting" involves the confirmation of one's partner as existing for him or herself, as "elementally other"; 2) The recognition of "otherness" is formative for personal identity; 3) Reciprocity is essential to all relationships; 4) There is a "sphere of the between" in

which two "others" meet and in their togetherness map out new territory;
5) Knowledge and meaning are confirmed and created in a relationship of real
meeting; 6) There is no absolute, exclusive, or final revelation to which
humans have access; and 7) Because there are no absolute dogmas, the mood
of life is one of "holy insecurity"; what sustains life is not knowledge of absolute
Truth but relationships of togetherness in which new truths arise. These, then,
are the elements which define Buber's approach to non-Jewish traditions—
notions which are affirmative of veridical pluralism and which invite mutually
transformative dialogue.

Unlike Rosenzweig, Buber does not controvert his own method by lifting
Judaism out of the realm of interhuman relations and onto the plane of the
eternal. In fact, Buber emphasizes the this-worldly character of Judaism,
exalting concrete, daily life as the arena in which dialogue occurs. In part,
Buber argues for the "hiddenness" of the messianic process, a hiddenness
which insures the continuity of daily life. Sacred and profane should not be
seen as ingredients of two different worlds, but as parts—redeemed and
unredeemed—of the one world. Moreover, it is life-in-community that fosters
the "world of unity," and the sort of community he has in mind is one in which
theological concerns are not removed from political concerns. By affirming
Judaism's connectedness to the temporal world, Buber stresses the imperative
nature of Judaism's involvement in the dialogic process.

Buber acknowledges Jesus as "my great brother"[105] and enjoins Jews to
make a place for Jesus within Jewish history. But it is in his call for a reconsideration of Judaism in light of the Christian emphasis on personhood that the
radical consequences of Buber's thought are manifested most clearly. I quote
again the important passage to which I refer:

> . . . an Israel striving after the renewal of its faith through the rebirth of the
> person and a Christianity striving for the renewal of its faith through the rebirth
> of nations would have something as yet unsaid to say to each other and a help to
> give one another—hardly to be conceived at the present time.[106]

The great disappointment is that, having developed the method and pointed to
a significant area of application, Buber does not undertake any further elaboration of his insight. He does not directly engage in transforming Judaism in
response to his encounter with other traditions. Indeed, despite Buber's ability
to enter into transformative dialogue, he does not do so in any sustained way.

To explain why not, one need only consider the social milieu in which Buber
lived and wrote. Is it not too much to expect Buber to celebrate the wisdom of
Christianity for Judaism at a time when the Christian mission to Judaism was
fervent and then later, when antisemitism was most inflamed? And aside from
these considerations, overwhelming though they may be, there is a further

explanation within Buber's own thought for his reluctance to act on his insight: his hypostatization of the Jewish people.

Jewish peoplehood is Buber's answer to the questions of why Judaism ought to survive in the twentieth century and how it might do so. According to Buber, the proper model for human existence is life-in-community and Jewish peoplehood is the example par excellence of that structure. The unit of human life is not the solitary individual but the individual-in-community. ". . . [P]eoplehood is the presupposition of the *whole* human response to God,"[107] and Jewish peoplehood is the "prototype" for this response. It is when Buber attributes personal existence to the Jewish people, when he treats the collective as a true individual with a genetic heritage as well as a religio-political one — with an unbroken and unbreakable relationship with God — that he steps out of the dialogical framework he has created. In essence, he finds a security for Judaism that violates his notion of "holy insecurity." When Buber argues that the immediacy with which the Jewish people is related to God qualifies the community as a whole and, despite external appearances, ever-characterizes the relationship, he provides a surety for Judaism which minimizes the need for Jews to seek truth in the truths of others. Especially when Buber criticizes Christianity for its lack of peoplehood and immediacy — the two attributes upon which Judaism's confidence is based — he undermines the desire and necessity for Jews to approach Christianity in a radically open way.

I do not mean to minimize the external events which may have affected Buber's actual encounter with non-Jewish traditions; nor do I wish to minimize Buber's great contributions to interreligious relations. Indeed, the barrier to transformative dialogue within Buber's understanding of Judaism can, I believe, be easily overcome. There is a way to talk about "community" without falling into the abstraction of "peoplehood" and losing the concrete, historical, nonabsolute, nonmonolithic character of life lived in intimate relationship with others. The Hasidic communities of Eastern Europe (as Buber understood them) served as Buber's paradigm for the individual-in-community and for life lived in "holy insecurity." His notion of "peoplehood" differs unnecessarily from the image of "community" derived from Hasidism.

Of the thinkers considered in this study, it is Buber who is best able to acknowledge the theological importance of other traditions for the self-understanding of Judaism and who moves farthest in that direction. When Buber writes about the Christian claim for Jesus' messiahship and declares that, "for his [Jesus'] sake *and my own*, I must endeavor to understand,"[108] he shows himself to be open to the transformative nature of dialogue. The religious claims of others, in particular of Christians, are, for Buber, claims upon himself, upon his life as a Jew. In recognizing that "we serve separately and yet all together,"[109] he does not avoid confrontation with those whose beliefs negate his own; nor does he seek a common ground of understanding which passes over the serious differences between traditions. What Buber acknowledges are the limitations of our human perspectives: Truth is greater than my perspective or yours, and therefore it is imperative that we join together to enlarge our perspectives and thus our understanding of truth.

6

Mordecai Kaplan: Co-inclusive Civilizations

In a tribute, Mordecai Kaplan praises Martin Buber for having fulfilled the "legitimate task of the theologian": to "transpos[e] the idiom of a religious tradition into the thought-pattern of one's contemporaries."[1] In so defining the theological task, Kaplan — the founder of Jewish Reconstructionism — reveals his own life's project and intellectual bias more accurately than that of Buber's.

Buber's work cannot be reduced to the formulation of "some acceptable idiom into which to transpose the beliefs, values, ideals and norms" of the Jewish past.[2] Above all, Buber was concerned with "religiosity," with the immediate, personal, dialogical relationship between the individual-in-community and God. Unlike Buber, Kaplan does not distinguish between religiosity and religion, between the spontaneous, creative event and the "organized," objectified form of that experience. That the distinction is not important to Kaplan is best illustrated by what he calls a "Copernican revolution" in the understanding of Judaism. What Kaplan "discovered" is that throughout Jewish history, the "central reality" of Judaism has been the Jewish people, not the Jewish religion per se. The traditional formulation, that the people serve the religion and that the religion literally "inspires" (that is, brings life into) the people, is reversed. Kaplan contends that "the Jewish religion must be maintained in order that the people may live" and *not* that the people should survive for the sake of the religion.[3] Judaism is to be understood as an evolving civilization, expressive of the life that Jews have lived and are living. Religion is *one* element of that life, unique to the civilization, but not the reason for the civilization.

It is by means of this "Copernican revolution" that Kaplan finds what he believes to be an idiom appropriate to the modern, scientific worldview. He rejects the "mythological and metaphysical types of religion," the former because of its superstitions and supernaturalism, the latter because of its emphasis on theories and proofs, on "abstractions from reality." In their stead he offers "scientific" religion: "religious humanism." This type of religion is not concerned "to give a metaphysical conception of God, but to make clear what we mean by the belief in God, from the standpoint of the difference that belief makes in human conduct and striving."[4] The theological task for Kaplan is different from that undertaken by Buber, as well as by Rosenzweig and Baeck, fundamentally because Kaplan's Judaism is not God-centered but people-centered.[5]

Indeed, Kaplan's thought has been characterized by one of his students as "really not a theology at all but an account of the psychological and ethical consequences of having one."[6] Kaplan, of course, has a metaphysics, just as all social scientists have a metaphysics, implicit and undeveloped as it may be. And he has a God-concept. But neither philosophy nor theology per se are on Kaplan's agenda. Kaplan conceives of religion in functional and pragmatic terms and as one element in the overall configuration of a people. Theological issues are superceded by sociological concerns.

In his many efforts to "transform Jewish life from a liability, which so many Jews think it is, into an asset,"[7] Kaplan rarely extends his discussion beyond the boundaries of Judaism. The making or remaking of Judaism into an asset does not, for him, include an extended comparison between Judaism and other faiths. The revitalization of Judaism depends on the reinterpretation and modernization of all the components which make up the Jewish civilization. The task is primarily an internal one.

Nevertheless, Kaplan does come to some conclusions about the relationship of civilizations to each other, with Judaism as his model for these relationships. Kaplan devotes himself to responding to the challenge that modernity poses to Judaism — not only the challenges of science, evolution, psychology, anthropology, and sociology, but also those posed by democracy and nationalism. In every case he assumes that modernity has something important to say to Jews and that Judaism, if it is to remain viable, must accept and adjust to these new insights.[8] Although he does not take up the subject of interreligious or intercultural dialogue directly, Kaplan reaches a position on the relationship of Judaism to the non-Jewish world through a discussion of these secular topics.

Judaism as a Civilization

Kaplan's pragmatic orientation is apparent from the first in the question he holds to be fundamental: How is Jewish survival to be secured in the twentieth century? In asking "how" instead of "why," Kaplan distinguishes himself from all post-Emancipation thinkers (other than certain Zionists) who saw their task and dilemma to be the justification of Judaism in light of modern philosophy, psychology, and science. For these thinkers, the survival of Judaism depended on whether they could adequately answer those who urgently asked, "Why should one be a Jew today?" As Kaplan notes, the assumption was that Judaism differed from other traditions solely in terms of religion; the solution, then, was to make the Jewish *religion* compatible with modern schools of thought and thus insure its validity. For Kaplan, as for his pre-Emancipation forbears, the existence of the Jewish people is an historical fact and, as such, needs no justification. The existence of a civilization is simply a "given." To ask why it should exist is wrongheaded and unnatural. In asking "how" Judaism is to continue before answering "why," Kaplan points back to such medievalists as Judah Halevi, for whom the "why of Judaism" was rendered moot by the brute fact of Jewish existence. At the same time, Kaplan attempts a solution to the very modern conditions which threaten Jewish survival.[9]

In his "solution," Kaplan weds pragmatism with functionalism. The purpose of any religion is to aid in the survival and growth of the people to whom it is indigenous. According to Kaplan, the key to a society's survival is the success it has in providing its members with the experience of life as worthwhile and meaningful, that is, with "salvation." Religion is the primary way in which the salvific demands of people are met by society because it is the "truest index" of the civilization's character. It is the "most self-conscious" element of a civilization, expressive of the character of the civilization.[10] But it is a reflexive rather than a creative agent, "inevitably determined by the context of the collective experience of the group."[11] Religion illuminates the actual, not the ideal. Neither the content nor the form of religion is the result of a supernatural revelation; religion is the outgrowth of a group of people who have consciously or unconsciously committed themselves to an existence together. It functions as the "collective soul or spirit" of the people who are, above all, concerned with group survival and hence the attainment of "salvation."[12]

> A religion thus came to mean to me [Kaplan] the sum of those habits and values which give a people the will to live in common, to perpetuate itself and to make the best use of its collective life. In achieving these results a people wins salvation.[13]

Religion, variously spoken of as an expression of the quest for salvation, as a means of achieving salvation, and as an element that insures group survival, is in every case no more than a lady-in-waiting to the reigning civilization. Jewish religion itself, then, is not the answer to the question of Jewish survival in the twentieth century. It is a part of the answer — indeed, a rather important part. The answer must be spoken, however, by the civilization as a whole, by that which is so much greater than any of its parts.

Kaplan's description of religion as the collective self-expression of a society's will-to-live clearly owes much to Emile Durkheim's evaluation of religion as a sociological construct. Kaplan terms his approach to religion "intuitional" and contrasts it with the approaches of revelation and rationalism. Religion in service to the larger social structure has no independent motivation and requires no justification of its own; it does not need to attach itself to a set of universal values or to a revelatory story. Instead, its purpose is intuited by the individual from the surrounding culture in which the same purposes — group identification, unity, and salvation — are expressed in a multitude of ways.

Though unarticulated, this awareness is the ultimate basis of religion, with philosophical and theological explanations offered as mere "formal after-thoughts." For example, according to Kaplan the power of the *Shema*, the Jewish prayer considered to be the "watchword of the faith," is derived not from what it proclaims—the oneness of God—but from what it evokes: "the thrill of being a Jew."[14] The same psycho-functional interpretation is given to religious observances and to the belief in God:

> The religious observances, too, claimed the fervent loyalty of the Jew primarily because they were a unique way of collective self-expression. What often passes for orthodoxy is a mode of Jewish life that is not motivated by a conviction of the supernatural origin of those observances . . . [but whose] chief purpose was to be identified with the Jewish people . . .[15]

> The God-idea in every collective religion functions not as an intellectual assent to a proposition, but as an organic acceptance of certain elements in the life and environment of the group, or of reality as a whole in its relation to the group, as contributing to one's self-fulfillment or salvation.[16]

Religion, including belief in God, finds its reason for being not in miracles, theophanies, logic, or tradition, but in the civilization of which it is a part.[17]

Because religion is simply a more intense expression of the civilization's purposes, the lines between religion and other cultural forms and between religion and civilization-in-general are often blurred. Religion is not alone in fostering group self-consciousness—indeed, it is dependent upon the commonality provided by extra-religious interests.[18] The relationship between all the elements of a civilization—language, literature, art, ethics, law, and so forth—is an organic one, based on the shared goal of providing the individual in the society with a meaningful and fulfilling life. Religion is distinct from these other components in the way it highlights the values and aims of the civilization and in the symbols it uses to promote the welfare of the culture-at-large. And it is religion that enables a civilization to reach "the point of self-consciousness essential to its perpetuation." For this very reason, however, religion must be tempered by the secular elements of society: "Preoccupation with religion, like preoccupation with oneself, is a form of morbidity."[19]

Excessive self-consciousness arising from an absorption in religion is a form of morbidity because it interferes with the overall development of the life of the organism. According to Kaplan, human life is naturally dependent on society for salvation, and therefore the normal unit of human life is peoplehood or civilization. Religion supports this communal structure by fostering group self-consciousness—necessary for human salvation—and by offering models of meaning for the society. But, he maintains, religion that is unloosed from the interconnections of society, or religion that operates hierarchically rather than organically within society, subordinating the other elements of a civilization to its interpretations, undercuts its own salvific efforts. By devaluing the secular elements of the society, attention is turned to other-worldly existence, to an ideology which offers human fulfillment not in the world-that-is but in the world-to-come. The result is an inability to respond to novelty and hence a weakening of the society's power to survive. Thus, Kaplan concludes that *"Paradoxical as it may sound, the spiritual regeneration of the Jewish people demands that religion cease to be its sole preoccupation."*[20]

Central, then, to Kaplan's "Copernican revolution" concerning Judaism is the idea that the Jewish religion, like all other religions, is *"a function of group life"* whose purpose is to serve the people by satisfying their spiritual needs.[21] Religion is no longer God-centered, but human-centered; its language is psychology not metaphysics; its goal is the fulfillment of human needs, not divine commands. And since human beings cannot achieve authentic fulfillment except amidst a body of people, the group or civilization is the primary enabler of fulfillment. Civilization, then, apart from any development or acquisition of a religious form per se, is itself a means of salvation; indeed it is *the* means of salvation for the individual. In developing or acquiring a religion, civilization does not become something more than it was; it merely becomes conscious of what it is. Kaplan reduces religion to a single, dependent, repetitious aspect of civilization. It is civilization, then, which deserves our attention as the elaborate record of the quest for human salvation.

According to Kaplan, a civilization is "the accumulation of knowledge, skills, tools, arts, literatures, laws, religions and philosophies which stands between man and external nature, and which serves as a bulwark against the hostility of forces that would otherwise destroy him."[22] It arises "organically," the outcome of generations of lives lived together. There is not one Civilization, but many civilizations or ways of life, each of which is, according to Kaplan, "a complete and self-contained entity."[23] This is the category under which Judaism — and Christianity and Islam — are to be understood. Any category that is less inclusive — Judaism as a revealed religion or Judaism as ethical monotheism — is an abstraction of Judaism designed to justify its existence according to the terms of particular periods of time. But Judaism, like all other civilizations, needs no justification, or rather is its own justification.[24]

Civilizations represent "unique *forms* of experience." The crucial differences between them lie not necessarily in their experiences but in the form these experiences take, especially the "non-transferable" forms of "language, literature, arts, religion and laws."[25] Indeed, the essence of a civilization is in its forms and hence it is not possible for one civilization to accommodate another civilization without a breakdown of one set of forms.[26] Kaplan argues that "difference" does not necessarily imply "unlikeness" — that is, "difference in quality;" instead, it is simply "otherness" — "difference in entity."[27] Civilizations are primarily "other" than one another and only secondarily, often superficially, "unlike" one another.

Judaism, as a civilization, is the "sum of *everything* about the Jewish people, past, present and future, which makes of the Jews a distinct and identifiable society."

> It consists of language, literature, history, laws, mores, folkways, ethical norms and ideals, all of which have their roots in Eretz Yisrael (the Land of Israel) and are related to the purpose of individual and collective salvation, thereby attaining religious significance.[28]

The Jewish civilization is something one is born into and which one absorbs with every sense; it is something one cannot take leave of without becoming a stranger to oneself. To be loyal to the Jewish civilization means, above all, to "express the will to *live*" as a Jew and the "will to belong to the Jewish people," both of which assume commitment to the survival of Judaism.[29]

What is striking about Kaplan's definition of Judaism-as-a-civilization and his understanding of what it means to be a Jew, is the absence of theology and philosophy as significant elements. Even on the topic of God, Kaplan abandons theology and philosophy and argues that he is entirely in line with tradition in doing so:

> What God was, metaphysically or ontologically, mattered only to a few intellectuals now and then. But what God meant morally, socially, economically, politically mattered to all of Israel's leaders, beginning with Moses.[30]

Indeed, Kaplan does not equivocate about his disinterest in questions of truth: "Judaism as a civilization is not a form of truth but a form of life."[31] As such its first priority is survival, followed by the ongoing effort to secure for its people a life in which they might realize their potential ever more fully. Toward this end — salvation in terms of human fulfillment through community — it is not important what people believe but how they feel and whether their feelings contribute to society's well-being.

There are, then, no dogmas to which Jews must univocally assent: indeed, doctrinal accord, rather than being necessary to the survival of the civilization, is actually counter to it. The effort to achieve complete agreement on the content of Jewish belief violates the organic character of Judaism in two important ways: it gives dogma a status above that of other cultural elements and thus lessens the richness and complexity of the civilization; and it replaces the will-to-belong with the need-to-believe and thus emphasizes duty to the self above allegiance to the community. An emphasis on dogma goes against what Kaplan believes to be the psychological deep structure of religion: "loyalty to one's historical community."[32] Needless to say, Kaplan understands the historic community to be much more than a cluster of cognitive claims about religion.

There are pragmatic arguments as well against a consensus on dogma (and these may well be Kaplan's first line of reasoning). The formation of a unified though diverse Jewish community, made up of Orthodox, Conservative and Reform Jews, would represent a considerable move toward strengthening Jewish life and thus improving the odds for group survival.[33] But the doctrinal differences between the Orthodox, Conservative and Reform communities are not likely to be overcome; these are the very differences that account for "what was once the most cohesive solidarity in the world" becoming "a kind of human rubble."[34] Kaplan maintains, however, that there is yet a binding thread that secures the fabric of Judaism: the ultimate concern of all Jews with the survival and advancement of the Jewish people. This thread will be the warp of a new fabric whose texture is not dogma but land, language, literature and the many interests and purposes that all Jews share. Kaplan also argues that Jews must affirm religious pluralism within their own community as a standard of democracy and as a security for Jewish equality within the non-Jewish world. Furthermore, Kaplan argues that since religion serves a psychological purpose — affirming life's worthwhileness — rather than a philosophical or theological purpose, it is not something that must be accepted or rejected. There is a third alternative, and that is to regard religion as "a symbol for spiritual desideratum in the present."[35]

The differences between civilizations, then, will not be found through a comparative study of their creeds and catechisms, general principles or ideologies. In one civilization there will almost certainly be a number of competing creeds and, at any rate, the unique character of a civilization is not best expressed in this way. The voice of a civilization does not limit itself to words, but speaks in terms of objects and associations related to the collective pursuit of salvation. Kaplan calls this constellation of group-specific forms *sancta*.

The sancta of a civilization include the people, places, events, objects, stories, celebrations, and other associations that "occupy a place of supreme value in the collective consciousness"[36] of a people. Among the sancta that are particular to the Jewish civilization are the land of Israel, the Torah scroll, Moses, Passover, and the covenant between God and the Jewish People. As both product of and descriptive of the group's particular history, they contribute to the cohesion and self-understanding of the group. Since religion is an intensification of the salvific impulses of the civilization as a whole, the sancta of a civilization are often the same as the religious symbols and are sacred to the civilization for the same reason that they are sacred to the religion — because of their power to give meaning to the people's existence and thereby to realize the salvific purposes of the civilization.

Kaplan's notion of sancta helps to clarify his understanding of the role of religion in a civilization. It is not the personal encounter with ultimacy or the lonely search for salvation in the traditional sense; nor is it the fulfillment of a personal vision of reality, mystical or metaphysical. It is, rather, "folk," "historical," or "group" religion, and is shaped by and for a civilization. Its language is the language of sancta and its goal is to participate in the meaning-giving life of the community. Folk religion, then, differs in important ways from "personal" religion: In addition to being embedded in a civilization it is, like language, a symbol-system which is transmitted at an unconscious and nonvoluntary level to the child; its authority is located in the group; it is highly particularistic, concerned with the survival and salvation of the people who adhere to it; and it consists originally and primarily of "group habits" (sancta) rather than "well-defined ideas." "The difference between a philosophic and a historic religion is like the difference between the general principles of a symphonic structure and the Ninth Symphony of Beethoven."[37]

Because it is not an outgrowth of any particular race, nationality, or history, personal religion can be fitted into any civilization as a "supplement" to the folk religion.[38] But it may not displace folk religion, for to substitute general principles for concrete particularities would mean the death of the civilization. "A folk religion is like the soul of a human being." Through it a coherent whole is formed and individual members find a sustained and harmonious relationship to it. And like the soul of a human being, a folk religion that passes from its indigenous civilization into an adoptive civilization acts like a dybbuk, speaking "with a voice not its own" and engaging in strange "antics."[39] Folk religion and its sancta, like self-consciousness and the soul, are not transferable elements of a civilization.[40]

The primary function of historical religions such as Judaism and Christianity is to sanctify the specific elements within the civilization that contribute to the self-fulfillment or salvation of both the individual and the group. "A group religion is least of all a *philosophy* of life."[41] It is most concerned with attaching the highest degree of emotional significance to the concrete particularities encountered by the group. Group religions differ from one another not in the measure of truth they possess but in the different constellations of sancta to which they adhere. Hence the essential difference not only between Samaritans and Jews but also between Jews and Christians is the difference of sancta.

It is interesting to note how the mere fact that the Samaritans insisted upon having their sanctuary at Mount Gerizim was enough to constitute them adherents of a different religion from the Jewish. Likewise Christianity branched off from the Jewish religion by adding the person of Jesus to the other Jewish *sancta*, though the early Christians, as is known, conformed to Jewish rites, accepted all the beliefs and honored all the *sancta* of the Jewish religion. It was a correct instinct which guided the church to declare the first instead of the seventh day holy, for if the church had observed the same day, its religion would not have been sufficiently distinct from the religion of the Jews.[42]

Civilizations differ from one another primarily in terms of their symbol systems, in the language they use to describe the world. They do not necessarily differ in their understanding of reality or in their interpretations of truth. Truth is universal and equally accessible to all people. However, it cannot be discovered in the abstract but only through the lights and shadows of the civilization in which one lives. Collective experience is the mediator of truth (as well as salvation). Truth, then, can be ascertained and expressed only through the development and interpretation of the group's sancta.[43] Universalism requires particularism.

The Jewish Civilization in Relationship with other Civilizations

Kaplan sets new parameters for the concepts of civilization, religion, and Judaism and arrives at an understanding of Judaism that is unique among modern Jewish thinkers. Likewise, the position he reaches on Jewish-non-Jewish relations has no parallel among his Jewish contemporaries. There are two outstanding features of his position: 1) His rejection of the concept of chosenness and his concomitant advocacy of relativism, and 2) His promotion of civil religion as a valid and inevitable complement to historical religion.

On Chosenness and Relativism

Kaplan lists the following as premises of a religion that is both universalistic and historical:

1) All men and peoples are in need of salvation.
2) All groups seek salvation in accordance with their own collective experience and by utilizing their own respective cultures.
3) The ultimate salvation of mankind depends on the recognition that no people can attain full salvation until all peoples attain it.
4) All peoples can attain salvation only when it is recognized that God is equally accessible to all religious groups through the development and interpretation of their own *sancta*.[44]

It is through the particular sancta of a group that God's presence and God's unity are affirmed and realized. We may not look forward to an ideal time when there will be one universal religion, but rather we should hope for the day when there will be many universalistic religions, each clothed in its unique sense of history. All religions are not "fundamentally" one, in spite of the fact that they are all expressive of the same universal truths and ideals. For Kaplan, what is fundamental to a religion is not its world outlook, but the sancta that are unique to each faith. Again utilizing the analogy of collective religion to the human mind, Kaplan writes, "Each group religion is different in substance or entity from every other group religion, as one mind is different from another. The *raison d'etre* of the existence of separate minds is by no means their logical diversity."[45] Religions differ because their sancta differ and because they serve groups of people which differ from one another without being "logically unlike" one another.

There are two radical affirmations concerning interreligious relations that Kaplan is able to make because of this position: First, non-Jewish religions are valid in and of themselves, apart from their adherence to any universal code such as the Noachide Laws. "The soul [that is, religion] of each [civilization] is equally precious in the sight of God."[46] Second, and related, Kaplan can argue that because religions do not "vary in the degree and truth that they express but in the group sancta,"—because they differ existentially but not propositionally—there is no logical basis for any claim to the inherent superiority of one religion over another.[47] All religions, insofar as they aid their parent civilizations in the quest for salvation, primarily through the sanctification of significant elements of group experience, are equally valid agents of meaning and truth.

Hence the traditional notion of Israel's divine election is vigorously and repeatedly rejected by Kaplan, who charges that it is both rationally and pragmatically untenable.

> Rationally it has no place in a universe of discourse from which belief in the supernatural revelation of religious truth is excluded. Pragmatically it is objectionable as barring the way to peace and harmony among religions and making for self-righteousness and cant.[48]

According to Kaplan, the idea of a chosen people, be it Jewish or Christian, is rooted in religious supernaturalism, which is the "astrological" or "alchemical" stage of religion,[49] and the rejection of chosenness goes hand-in-hand with the rejection of supernaturalism. Kaplan reproves Reform thinkers for retaining the idea of chosenness as a core notion, even in the reinterpreted form of mission. The literal form in which "Jews thank God that He has not made them like other nations, and the Christians declare the Jews to be the rejected of God,"[50] so dominates the minds of Jews and Christians that it cannot be sufficiently transformed, but must be entirely rejected.

For Kaplan it is the concept of peoplehood that merits that seat held by the doctrine of chosenness.[51] Indeed, what chosenness is to supernatural religion, peoplehood is to "transnatural" religion. In religion that is "transnatural," God's presence is manifested in "the fulfillment of human nature," rather than in any interruption of natural processes.[52] It is, according to Kaplan, the only alternative to supernaturalism that is both entirely in line with the modern worldview and existentially satisfying. Through the notion of peoplehood, transnatural religion is able to fulfill what had been the primary function performed by supernatural religion: the need for assurance and the means to salvation. While modern science has led to a repudiation of supernatural events, modern psychology has achieved insight into the universal and instinctual needs of human nature. Above all, human beings have a need to be fulfilled, and it is "the inescapable law of human nature that only through interaction with his group can the individual achieve personality and self-fulfillment or salvation."[53] Transnatural religion preserves the truth in the Chosen *People* doctrine — that the individual gains salvation within a specific group. But it is the group itself which enables the individual to fulfill his or her potential as a human being. Salvation comes through the people itself, not through the election of the people by God.

The focus on peoplehood rather than on divine election has two important consequences for the relationship between faiths. First, in freeing itself from the concept of chosenness, Judaism liberates itself from the defensive and contentious posture necessarily required by a claim to superiority. Kaplan holds that a "sense of consecration and responsibility"[54] can be had apart from the competition for ethical or philosophical superiority. Civilizations and their religions exist as the means for *a* people's fulfillment and the record of their achievement. As such they need not be justified either by those who stand within or to those who stand apart from that particular structure. As self-justifying institutions, civilizations define themselves in their own terms and can savor both their uniquenesses *and* their commonalities with other civilizations. Dialogue then loses its traditional offensive-defensive structure and the participants can encounter one another with a confidence in their own traditions that is not gained at the expense of another's.

Secondly, in substituting the concept of peoplehood for the concept of chosenness, Kaplan widens the region of our concern in regard to people of different faiths. The concept of peoplehood requires an affirmation of the comprehensive nature of human life. Under the rubric of peoplehood, it is not possible to limit our understanding of one another to an understanding only of each other's religion because religion cannot be abstracted out of its cultural matrix. It is the civilization which provides religion with its substance and it is religion, in the main, which provides culture with its sancta. In order to establish a relationship between traditions, we must come to understand whole civilizations.

Kaplan, then, formulates a number of propositions that might initiate a new form of Jewish-non-Jewish relationship: he removes the stumbling block of chosenness and affirms that all properly functioning religions are valid; he argues that the test for validity rests within the particular civilization; he proposes the notion of peoplehood as the common ground for all particularistic religions; and he calls upon us to consider the larger matrix within which religion abides. It comes as a surprise, then, to find that Kaplan himself does not intentionally further interreligious or intercultural discussion.

To understand why not, one must examine the psychological model that underlies Kaplan's understanding of religion and culture. Human beings are defined by their personalities, which are, in turn, shaped by the collective personality; personhood is peoplehood. Since religion is the "collective personality" of a people, it is only through that particular personality that an individual in a civilization can achieve spiritual satisfaction. Furthermore, Kaplan's "psychological point of view" leads him to a position of cultural and religious relativism. Hence there is nothing to be gained from an interreligious or intercultural discussion on any level, and particularly on the theological level, when adherence to a tradition is pure psychological necessity.

In answer to the modern question, Why be a Jew? — a query which assumes the voluntary nature of religious adherence — Kaplan echoes an old-world order in which the corporate and non-voluntary nature of religious adherence was assumed: "Be a Jew because that is the civilization into which you were born." This is only a slightly updated version of the traditional birth dogma. Cultural relativism reinforced by psycho-social determinism is barren soil for interreligious or intercultural exchange.

The civilization into which one is born determines one's identity, which cannot be communicated fully to those who do not participate in the same self-consciousness; collective personality is as private as individual personality. What religions "mean to their own members and what they mean to others can never be the same, any more than I can mean to you what I mean to myself."

> Thus, if a devout Christian tells me that he finds in the adoration of the personality of Jesus all the inspiration that he requires for living a life that satisfies his spiritual needs, I cannot as a Jew say this attitude is not true, although I am so conditioned that I could not possibly find it true in my own experience. . . . Since his religion is not a part of the Jewish civilization that has conditioned my thinking and feeling, and my religion is not a part of the Christian civilization which has conditioned his, comparison between the two is meaningless.[55]

Religions and the civilizations to which they belong are closed systems. They are self-justifying, self-sufficient, and nontransferable systems, concerned not with the promotion of truth but with the preservation of their ways of life. Thus it is not useful, or even possible, to measure the qualities of one civilization or religion against another. A religion is true insofar as it is true for the individual who asserts its truth. And it is true for an individual insofar as it is an expression of the civilization which the individual calls home.

The beauty of the psychological approach to religion is that it engenders both firm commitment to the religion of one's birth and complete tolerance of religions other than one's own. The assertion that all religious traditions and the civilizations they represent are equal is, according to Kaplan, the basis for true religious tolerance, tolerance that insures the right to disagree as much as the right to agree.[56] Relativism is the logical consequence of Kaplan's religion-as-personality theory. Coupled with psycho-sociological determinism, it is Kaplan's solution to the dilemma of religious particularism in a modern world.

On Civil Religion

Just as the defining characteristics of civilization extend not only to political groups but to historic religions as well, Kaplan argues that the defining characteristics of folk religion apply not only to religious movements but also to national entities. "Civic loyalty which finds expression in patriotism," he claims, "is fundamentally a continuation of the role played by religions in the past. It is in large measure the modern form of folk religion."[57] In the same way that religion serves to unify the group, especially through the contribution of sancta, patriotism and the symbols it gives rise to provide the civic group with a program for social cohesion. Indeed, the roots of patriotism are the same as those of religion, for in the beginning, cultic life was structurally undifferentiated.

Through his psycho-social model of religion, augmented by the rejection of the doctrine of chosenness, Kaplan is able not only to recognize the existence of civil religion, but also to give a positive assessment of its functions. As the personality or soul of the collective, civil religion provides a structure for the moral and spiritual values of the group. It thereby instills within it a sense of unity and raises its life "to the level of cosmic significance." In American civil religion, for example—the only form to which Kaplan refers—democracy becomes a "faith to live by as well as to die for."[58] This degree of existential commitment rests on the ability of civil religion to provide its adherents with salvation. Indeed, Kaplan asserts, "Democracy is to us Americans nothing less than a method of this-worldly salvation."[59] Having determined that the means of salvation belongs to civilizations and then having reasoned that salvation is not the exclusive possession of one civilization, Kaplan reaches the conclusion that civic communities may be as valid and effective a source of salvation as historic religious civilizations.[60]

For interreligious relations, what is significant about Kaplan's affirmation of civil religion is his position that an individual may—indeed, in most cases must—live simultaneously in two civilizations. He argues for the recognition of "cultural hyphenism" as a "moral and spiritual right."[61] For people such as American Jews and Catholics, who belong to "minority civilizations," complete self-fulfillment cannot be attained apart from participation in the majority one. The historic religious civilization as the primary source of salvation is replaced in the age of nations by the national civilization in which the individual lives. "The Jew in America will be first and foremost an American, and only secondarily a Jew."[62] Given this new condition, historic religious civilizations must not demand the exclusive loyalty of the individual. At the same time, the majority civilization must grant legitimacy to the minority ones. Both civilizations must accept cultural hyphenation as a requirement of modern life.

Not only can a person be both a Jew and an American (or a Catholic and an American, and so forth)—a prominent concern in America during the first half of the twentieth century—but a person who adheres to a minority civilization must be able to maintain dual loyalties. "Indeed, the only way out of the present melee of historical civilizations and modern nationalities is to sanction the necessity of living in more than one civilization. That is the inevitable lot of the modern man."[63] In suggesting that an individual must live in two civilizations at once, Kaplan extends the level of tolerance from that of the mere coexistence of different civilizations—the level reached in relativism—to that of co-inclusiveness. Civilizations that are co-inclusive work in complementary ways to bring about the salvation of the individual.[64]

As long as they do not contradict one another, that is, as long as their respective sancta do not compete with each other, neither civilization threatens the integrity of the other. Two civilizations can be co-inclusive without any forfeiture of their uniqueness. "Otherness" does not require "separation." On this principle, Kaplan sanctions the intermarriage of Jews with non-Jews, providing that "the homes they establish are Jewish and their children are given a Jewish upbringing."[65] It is not a law of nature that intermarriage must result in the death of Judaism, or in broader terms, that the minority civilization must always give way to the majority one.[66]

It is because Kaplan believes that civilizations subscribe to the same worldview that he can argue for cultural hyphenism.

> The difference in character between one civilization and another is not so much in the ideals they profess as in the social institutions they evolve as a means of expressing their ideals.[67]

Given this rather major assumption—that Western civilizations hold a common set of ideals—the crucial ingredient for a co-inclusive relationship is whether the sancta which define the civilizations are mutually complementary or, at the least, "mutually neutral." Kaplan makes the groundbreaking assertion that "there would be no paradox in being at the same time both a Christian and a Jew, if it consisted merely in living in two civilizations that are mutually neutral."[68] But he allows his understanding of the actual relationship between Jews and Christians to obscure the possibilities embodied in his model. Kaplan elaborates on this insight only to repudiate it.

. . . when one of the two civilizations is avowedly antagonistic to the other, a person imposes upon himself an intolerable conflict of loyalties by trying to live in both. The very existence of Judaism is regarded by Christianity and Moham- medanism [sic] as a challenge to their authority. The New Testament is no less interested in denouncing Judaism than in advancing its own ideas of what man must do to enter the Kingdom of God. It would therefore be the height of absurdity for a Jew to want to remain a Jew while subscribing to Christianity or Mohammedanism, just as it would be absurd for one to be a Christian and a Mohammedan at the same time.[69]

Elsewhere he makes the same claim, that the history of Jewish-Christian relations abolishes the viability of maintaining loyalty to both civilizations.

Without in any way derogating Christianity as a means to salvation for the Christian, the average Jew who would adopt it as an alternative to Judaism would be doing violence to his intellectual integrity. He would also commit himself to a communion whose religion is largely based on denouncing the People he was born into as deicides, or Christkillers, and as doomed to perdition.[70]

Kaplan explores the possibility of loyalty to both Judaism and Christianity no further. Nevertheless he creates an opening within the Reconstructionist movement for a revolutionary conception of the relationship between Jews and non-Jews. For example, if one were to maintain Kaplan's definition of historic religious traditions as civilizations and recognize that Christianity need not define itself over against Judaism,[71] then one could hold that it is possible to be both a Jew and a Christian. Or if one were to interpret New Testament antagonism toward Judaism as a consequence of Christianity's efforts to distinguish itself from the religion of Judaism and not from the civilization of Judaism — no different from the doctrinal disputes between Orthodox and Reform Jews — then one might conclude that Judaism and Christianity are two forms of the same civilization, that their commonalities far outweigh their differences, and that their sancta are not conflicting and often complementary. Kaplan offers a basis for making these sorts of pro- posals, but he does not pursue them.

Kaplan's personal mission is to make Judaism a viable option for twentieth- century Jews, and he recognizes that this involves interaction not only with the academic realms of science, psychology, and sociology, but with other civiliza- tions as well.

For Judaism to become creative once again, it must assimilate the best in contemporary civilizations. In the past this process of assimilating cultural ele- ments from the environment was carried on unconsciously. Henceforth that process will have to be carried on in deliberate and planned fashion. . . . It is in the spirit, therefore, of adopting the best in other civilizations and cooperating with them, and not in the spirit of yielding to their superior force or prestige, that Judaism should enter upon what will constitute a fourth stage in its development.[72]

What the method of this conscious exchange is to be does not receive much attention from Kaplan. That he does not consider formal dialogue between representatives of different civilizations to be a noteworthy arena for this exchange is not surprising given his relativism, his disregard for theology, and his overwhelming concern with questions of expediency rather than of truth.

For the most part, Kaplan offers no guidelines for absorbing the truth of other traditions or, for that matter, any reason to do so. A great irony of Kaplan's thought is that in his commitment to modernity and to constructing a Judaism in harmony with it, he reaches a position from which he cannot pursue the values of modernity to their fullest extent. In making group loyalty and understanding dependent on birth and in emphasizing group self-consciousness over individual development, Kaplan comes close to promoting racialism (without the claims for superiority), and racialism is nonvoluntary, radically particularistic, and (in the long run) a negation of the profoundly social nature of reality. In arguing for relativism, Kaplan reaches a level of tolerance that is in fact inconsistent with his pragmatic goals: relativism, because it does not encourage people to understand one another in any serious way, is finally no insurance against intolerance. Perhaps more importantly, relativism cuts off the exploration of imaginative possibilities that might emerge in the overlap between two traditions, the sort of possibilities that Kaplan sees as necessary to the revitalization of Judaism and which he intuits in his call for cultural hyphenism.

Kaplan's commitment to Judaism exceeds his commitment to any particular intellectual construct, and it is this that accounts for the frequent inconsistencies in his thought.[73] But it is Kaplan's idea of the co-inclusiveness of civilizations that is most promising for inter-cultural relations and that is, finally, most in accord with Kaplan's goals — the survival and advancement of Judaism in twentieth-century America.

Critical Reassessment

Kaplan's relativism, ethnocentrism, and lack of regard for theological concerns would seem not to make him a very good candidate for participation in mutually transformative dialogue. These aspects of his thought, accepted in their most extreme form and without qualification by other aspects, seriously limit his contributions in this area. On the other hand, his repudiation of the notion of chosenness, his advocacy of "cultural hyphenism," his promotion of the communal nature of religion, and his rejection of theological dogmatism are all consonant with the development of transformative dialogue. Indeed, when these aspects of his thought are joined with a tempered version of relativism, ethnocentrism, and theological indifference, much can be said on behalf of Reconstructionism as a form of Judaism that is strongly affirmative of veridical pluralism.

Kaplan's central assertion is that Judaism is not merely a religion but that it is an evolving civilization. In recognizing that religion is not separate from other aspects of culture and that it is embedded in an historical matrix, Kaplan is able to leave behind the idea of an absolute form of Judaism and to appreciate the introduction of novelty into it. If civilizations are to be understood as organic forms of life, then growth and change must be seen as processes essential to the health of the organism. Nothing, especially not dogmatic propositions, must interfere with the ability to survive and, beyond that, to flourish. Because there is no attachment to dogmatic formulations, Reconstructionists are able to approach the truths which may reside in non-Jewish traditions without the defensiveness that usually marks the Jewish-non-Jewish encounter. Reconstructionism is not limited to a reconstruction of traditional Judaism; it invites a continual reconstruction of itself. Certainly this feature of Kaplan's thought fits well with the model of transformative dialogue.

Among the reasons why Kaplan rejects the notion of chosenness is his belief that "God is equally accessible to all religious groups through the development and interpretation of their own sancta"; all religions and the civilizations to which they are linked may be positive vehicles for salvation.[74] And although he also maintains that the difference between these salvific vehicles is not their "logical diversity" but their sociological configurations, Kaplan vehemently rejects the search for one common approach to salvation. In fact, it is not clear why Kaplan minimizes the differences between civilizations, calling them facts of "otherness" rather than facts of "unlikeness."[75] Kaplan is in the position to affirm much deeper differences than those of simple "otherness."

The two major obstacles to Kaplan's participation in dialogue are his extreme ethnocentrism and his relativism. Ethnocentrism, as Kaplan explains the concept, makes it impossible to exchange ideas; relativism makes it unnecessary to do so. Kaplan does not consider any alternative to absolutism other than relativism, but the alternative, which undergirds transformative dialogue—absolute commitment to being responsive to life as it evolves[76]—seems to be quite in line with Reconstructionism as a whole. And within his own thought, Kaplan's ethnocentrism comes into conflict with his call for cultural hyphenism, for life lived simultaneously within two (or more) civilizations. If civilizations are truly self-enclosed and nontransferable, then co-inclusive living calls for schizophrenia. But this is finally not Kaplan's position. As long as the sancta of the civilizations are "mutually neutral"—and they may be complementary—Kaplan holds that it is possible and *desirable* for the individual to participate in both civilizations. He also recognizes that it is imperative for Judaism to consciously "assimilate the best in contemporary civilizations."[77] In his call for cultural hyphenism, Kaplan overcomes his radical ethnocentrism and creates a very promising opening for the transformative growth of religions and their civilizations.

The modifications of Reconstructionism that are suggested here are not minor ones, but neither are they incompatible with its basic tenets. Kaplan creates a mood for transformative dialogue, although he does not pursue it. However, when some elements of his system are qualified by others, Kaplan offers us a context in which transformative dialogue can occur.

7

Toward Mutually Transformative Dialogue: The Example of Judaism and Buddhism

The promise that God makes with Abraham, revealing that Abraham's descendants will be accorded much value, is given two translations in the Revised Standard Version of the Bible:

. . . by you all the families of the earth shall bless themselves.

. . . in you all the families of the earth shall be blessed.[1]

The difference between the two lines is expressive of the difference between dialogue that is not transformative and dialogue that is. The first lacks the necessary degree of mutuality — the movement of blessing is one-directional, from Abraham's descendants to the other nations. But in the second translation, the internality and mutuality of relations is evoked; the families of the earth will be a part of Israel, a part of the blessing that Israel becomes. It is this second translation that captures the direction of this essay.

Transformative dialogue is clearly an extension of appreciative dialogue. If we appreciate something about another religion, having recognized some value within it, then we must ask ourselves what becomes of that value within our own tradition. Unless value is transcendent of particular traditions, we are all prisoners of relativism. I am not speaking of value in any market sense, in which case it is more precise to speak of prices or cost benefits. I am speaking of intrinsic worth, apart from this or that particular cultural pattern. If we recognize that there is something worthy about another tradition and if we truly admit to its value, we must appraise ourselves in relationship to that value. Such a self-study, arising from the fact of our appreciation of another religion, may be transformative.

For the most obvious reasons, interreligious dialogue in the Jewish community has almost always been between Jews and Christians and for the most obvious and unfortunate reasons, that dialogue has often been rife with accusation, hyperbole, and a general lack of generosity and sympathy. For the past twenty-five years, however, some Christians have worked very hard to change the temper of Jewish-Christian relations. Many of these people enter into dialogue with a better understanding of Judaism in both its first-century and twentieth-century forms, and they tend to cherish the ties that bind their tradition to the Jewish one. But the sins of the past continue to trouble those who attempt today's dialogue, and there has not been enough time for a new relationship to form in which suspicions and accusations can be set aside.

The potential of transformative dialogue can be better demonstrated, therefore, if the obstacles which obstruct Jewish-Christian dialogue can be avoided. Thus, I have chosen instead to imagine an encounter between liberal Judaism and Buddhism. The histories, texts, and voices of these two significant traditions have been shaped without deference to each other. The possibility that two such different traditions would not have something important to say to one another seems rather remote. The recent flowering of scholarly interest in Buddhism and the current reaffirmation of the importance of interreligious dialogue make this a good time for Jewish thinkers to turn their attention to its traditions and to enter into meaningful exchange with adherents of its many forms.

Very little has been written about the relationship between these two traditions. Leo Baeck's discussion of Buddhism is representative of most nineteenth-century approaches to non-Western faiths: it is marred by a categorical misreading of the primary texts by Western Buddhologists of the day and limited by Baeck's own theological agenda. As indicated in chapter three, Baeck sees Buddhism as the complete antithesis of Judaism and thus mistaken about life in every way. For example, where others saw some overlap between Buddhism and Judaism on the doctrine of love, Baeck finds none.

> Buddhism's doctrine of love fondly preaches mercy and benevolence toward every living thing, but in its inner core this feeling is one of sentimentality and melancholy. It lacks the reverence for the fellow man which distinguishes Jewish teaching; it lacks the emphasis upon positive justice and hence the clear demand of the moral task. It lacks the great "Thou shalt," the imperative force and urgency, the social and the messianic elements which are emphasized by Judaism. Beyond mere feeling Buddhist morality does not go. That is what gives it its characteristically passive and negative stamp. For warmth of feeling without a definite commitment to duty is merely ethical inertia or idleness: to sympathize with the lot of our neighbor only in our heart means in practice to stand apart from him. That is why Buddhism has been termed the religion of inertia. That may seem a harsh judgment, but surely one aspect of it is true: Buddhism with all of its idealist merits is a religion of feeling without activity. And for it, like Christianity, salvation means everything; the question of the "I" is the sole question of life.[2]

Baeck's misreading of Buddhism is evident, especially in his assertion that "the question of the 'I' is the sole question of life." Buddhism does not speak of a substantial self and regards concern with ego to be illusory and a primary source of suffering. Also evident is Baeck's evaluation of Buddhism as the negation of all Jewish values. Here, and elsewhere, it is described as a religion of inertia, resignation, fatalism, superficiality, and moral vacancy.[3]

Martin Buber speaks with more familiarity and insight about Buddhism.[4] In his brief comparison of Zen Buddhism and Hasidism, Buber offers an excellent example of how to approach another tradition in a nonpolemical way. Although his final judgment is that Hasidism is a better expression of mysticism (indeed, the best expression there is), he reaches this conclusion without forcing an easy dichotomy between the traditions. Indeed, he begins by discussing the characteristics common to them both, in particular their essential agreement that "the key to truth is the next deed" and that this key is received only through lived experience. In Buber's estimation, however, Zen Buddhism shares the same deficiency as Christianity: it fails to sustain the dialogical principle. When the Zen monk seeks for enlightenment within his own nature, he engages in a monologue and the relational character of the universe is denied. And because such contemplation is ahistorical, Buber argues that Zen Buddhism empties concrete existence of its value and thus seeks "annulment" of time rather than "fulfillment" in time. In contrast, Hasidism is able to advance the dialogue because it maintains the distinction between the I and the Thou. "[E]ven the relationship of the most intimate reciprocity remains a relationship, the relation to a Being that cannot be identified with our being remains unshaken."[5] And because "in Israel all religion is history, including mystical religion," Hasidism succeeds in illuminating both the moment beyond time and historical time.[6] Buber thus concludes that Hasidism is superior to Zen Buddhism. It is a conclusion that requires further debate, especially in regard to Buber's understanding of the Buddhist notion of the no-self. But Buber's method and his tone enable us to continue the discussion.

In the following few pages, I shall give an example of what mutually transformative dialogue between a Buddhist and a liberal Jew *might* look like. What follows is a "thought experiment"; it is not the result of actual dialogue with Buddhist thinkers and therefore it is an intellectual construct and should be treated as such. But I believe that the exercise is valuable on that level — indeed, that such exercises can be propaedeutic to real dialogue.

Isaiah Ben-Dasan, a writer who was raised as a Jew in Japan, declares that "few peoples are as fundamentally dissimilar as the Japanese and the Jews."

> Indeed, readers who know one or the other of these peoples intimately may perhaps object that any comparison is impossible. As a Jew born and raised in Japan, I know both the Japanese and the Jews well, and I am only too keenly aware of the difficulties involved in comparing them if the aim of the examination is to discover similarities. There are simply too few to bother hunting for them.[7]

Ben-Dasan limits his analysis primarily to sociological, geographical and historical differences between the two cultures, and does not speak directly about religious differences, about which, however, the same can be said.

Speaking very broadly, Judaism might be described as a religion that is fundamentally concerned with the ethical and Buddhism fundamentally with the
aesthetic.

Although the statement that Judaism is primarily oriented toward the moral
dimension can be debated, there is much to support this generalization.
Indeed, Judaism as ethical monotheism is the definition most familiar to and
accepted by Reform Jews today. Even those who, like Buber, argue that
Judaism is primarily about the I-thou encounter, find a central place for the
concrete action which derives from that elementary divine-human experience.
The framework that supports this ethical orientation is the covenant.

One way to describe the covenant is as a contractual agreement, but this
language is too dry to capture the spirit of it. At Mt. Sinai a promise was
made, a promise that was secured by a covenant, and hence acquired a static
form, but which, in another sense, remained dynamic, addressing a promising
future. In its literal meaning, promise means "sending forward" (pro + mission), and it is this orientation toward the future that is crucial to a proper
understanding of the covenant. What is sent forward is a vision of how things
ought to be: Israel ought to be a holy nation, a kingdom of priests, and if the
people of Israel keep the covenant, they shall become holy. The fulfillment of
the covenant lies in the future and this fact was recognized from the start, for
the covenant was made "with him who is not here with us this day as well as
with him who stands here with us this day before the Lord our God" (Deut.
10:14–15). What the people of Israel committed themselves to when they
accepted the covenant was an understanding of reality as "promise-bearing,"
and in that way, as something unfulfilled. The people of Israel are a people
who have committed themselves to the not-yet.

This commitment has empowered the Jewish people. It has helped Jews to
endure the most awful of present moments, for it was believed that these
moments were somehow not fully real. Each moment had a context beyond its
own fierce pain, and that context prevailed over any momentary despair. "I
believe with perfect faith in the coming of the Messiah, and though he tarry,
nevertheless I believe" — this is what untold numbers of Jews have spoken in
the face of death. The meaning of the present does not repose wholly within
the present; something is absent from every moment of experience. Every
moment is a "not-yet," filled with the expectation of fulfillment.[8]

This understanding of the present as promise-laden has had enormous
impact on the structure of Judaism. The most obvious consequence is in terms
of the way history has been understood. History moves in a linear way, toward
a future that has been assured, but not yet secured. A deep sense of confidence
and optimism, unwarranted by daily events, undergirds Jewish life: the future
that most certainly will come promises to be good. Confidence that the future
will bring blessings does not, however, lead to a passive waiting for the end.
Passivity on the part of human beings would contravene the covenantal part-

nership. Instead, that confidence contributes to the energy with which Jews work to secure the future.

At the same time that the future is promised, there is yet the sense that change is not necessarily in the nature of things, that the future is not going to arrive as expected unless the individual works to make it happen. What the individual does, then, is of utmost concern. The promise will not be fulfilled apart from the human effort to fulfill it. The individual is therefore morally obligated to act in such a way that the covenantal promise is brought closer to fulfillment. From the Jewish perspective, the task of one who lives within this imperfect world is to change it, to make it more as it ought to be. The aim of Jewish life, then, is not to escape this world, but to sanctify it. The classical Jewish texts serve to teach the individual how to live in such a way that the moral order might be secured and the future "ought" made a reality. To interpret those texts as primarily legalistic is to abstract them from the covenantal worldview, in which the deed and the doer are both given careful attention because the future, with all its blessed promise, is believed to depend on them. In sum, Judaism's orientation toward the "not-yet" and toward the "ought to be" is expressed by its prevailing concern with ethics.

To say that Judaism centers on the ethical is a statement about the basic vision of the tradition and the structure that best expresses this vision. In the Jewish tradition, the covenantal vision of a future time when the world is as it should be is best expressed in an ethical structure. In Buddhism, on the other hand, the basic vision is of the wholeness of the present. Since the present is the really real, the Buddhist aims at a sensitive awareness of the immediate moment. It is thus an aesthetic approach that best expresses the Buddhist vision. While the Jew is oriented, by virtue of the covenant, to the "not-yet," the Buddhist focuses on the "here-now." For the Buddhist, the present does not rely upon something other than itself for its value; indeed, there is nothing but the present that exists. It does not make sense to say that the present lacks something as there is no ideal past or future against which it can be compared. The future is "not," the present "is" and is all that is. To live toward the future, or in the past, is to be disoriented. And such disorientation, rather than alleviating suffering, leads to suffering.

The idea that hope in the future (as well as delight in the past) causes the individual to suffer is in utter opposition to the Jewish worldview. For the Jew, the future makes the present more meaningful, more productive, and more bearable. For the Buddhist, living toward the future is without merit on at least three grounds. First, to make a future that does not exist one's polestar is to live a life of delusion. It is to cheat oneself of the only life there is, the momentary now. Second, to regard the future as something apart from the present is to destroy the unity of experience. It imposes a dualism on that which is temporally indivisible, and hence, again, it misconceives reality. Thirdly, and perhaps most importantly, living toward the future constitutes a form of clinging, and it is clinging or attachment that is the source of all suffering. When the Jew says, "I believe with perfect faith in the coming of the Messiah, and though he tarry, nevertheless I believe," the Buddhist does not hear this as a courageous affirmation of future redemption, but rather as that from which one needs to be redeemed. In the best and worst of times, Jews cling to the messianic hope, living this life in light of that which is to come. This attachment, and any other, the Buddhist argues, creates a false frame of reference by which the world is experienced. The moment which is its *own* center loses centrality; it is evaluated in terms of the attachment or the goal. So the present is experienced as that which serves something other than itself; in the case of Judaism, the present serves the future. The present, then, is undervalued; it becomes the arena of suffering because it is incomplete and hence unsatisfying.

For the Buddhist, it is the present moment itself that is promising. And if that promise is to be revealed, the individual must be fully present to the moment, *here*, present in the present. The individual must not separate his or her presence from the occasion that is coming to be, nor may the becoming moment be understood as anything other than for itself. When the here-now is no longer understood as could-be or should-be, but simply and completely as here-now, when one is freed from all false frames of reference, then life is felt in all its immediacy and fullness and there can be no dissatisfaction with it.

An ethical structure requires a sense of what could be, a vivid awareness of possibilities. It depends upon the experience that there is a causal connectedness of events and that certain possibilities are linked to certain past events. This is the structure that best describes Judaism. An aesthetic structure requires the experience of Gestalten in their immediate, emotional wholeness. It depends on a way of being that enables one to be fully present, vividly aware, and sensitive to the now and to nothing else. This is the structure that best describes Buddhism.

What is the relationship between these two approaches? Or, rather, what is one of the possible relationships between these two approaches? They begin with different valuations of time: Judaism is future-oriented, Buddhism is present-oriented. They emphasize different modes of experience: Judaism stresses the ethical, Buddhism the aesthetic. For those who orient their lives to the "not-yet," does an orientation to the "here-now" have something of value to contribute? Conversely, for those who live in terms of the "here-now," is there something of worth in an orientation toward the "not-yet"? Is there a way of holding the "not-yet" together with the "here-now?" To answer any of these questions with satisfaction requires a living dialogue between Jewish and Buddhist thinkers. What might result from such a dialogue may be very different from what I will propose. Affirmative responses, however, will not be gained unless the *possibility* that the two traditions have something of value to offer each other is granted.

I am convinced that in regard to the discussion of temporal orientation, Buddhism and Judaism might learn from each other. I believe that Buddhism would be enhanced if it were able to speak with greater clarity about the moral obligations that exist between one person and another, between this generation and the past, and between this generation and future generations. There is a way to talk about the future without obscuring the present and that is in terms of possibilities. Possibilities exist and with each new moment of experience, some possibilities die and others are born. There is a linkage between the now and the not-yet because the present moment affects the pool of possibilities that is available to the next present moment. Part of the here-now is the set of possibilities that it affirms and denies. To some extent, then, that-which-is involves that-which-will-be. If this link between the present and the future (the future by way of present possibilities) is acknowledged, then it becomes necessary to talk about what should be in addition to what is. There is, then, an opening for the ethical dimension in which there is both commitment to the present and responsibility for the future. For Buddhism to incorporate an emphasis on ethical activity would require a deep transformation. I cannot say how it should be done. But, speaking as a Jew, it seems to me that Buddhism would be better for such a change.

How might the self-understanding of Judaism be enriched through dialogue with Buddhism? Very briefly, I will argue that Judaism can learn from Buddhism's emphasis on the present moment; it can remember to reemphasize the beauty of this life and it can attempt to generate a better understanding of the relationship between the beautiful and the good.

Let me begin by asking the question, Why is there such a paucity of Jewish religious art? Although there are some wonderful examples of synagogue art, the visual arts are, on the whole, not emphasized in the Jewish tradition, the standard explanation being the biblical prohibition against making graven images. It strikes me, however, that this answer is not sufficient, and that a good part of the explanation is the Jewish orientation toward the future and its emphasis on the ethical dimension of life.

What is required of the artist is intense attention to the present moment. But if the present moment is understood not to be the central point of value, it is not deserving of such focus. Indeed, it can be said that such attentiveness is a form of idolatry, drawing us away from the promise—and substituting a partial joy for the full splendor of the messianic kingdom. Because the present is not whole, the individual who focuses on the aesthetic experience is limiting his or her awareness of reality.

In the most general terms, for the Jew the purpose of life is to serve God. In the service of God, one may very well experience beauty, but the aesthetic experience is subordinate to the duty of service. To truly experience life is to know and to do "what is required of thee," that is, to be just, merciful, and holy. In contrast, the Buddhist holds that a life rightly lived is akin to a work of art.

Buddhism is thus the celebration of the joy of living, the joy being the natural expression or "voice" of the vivid quality and heightened awareness flowing in those original centers of experience where life is becoming ever more fully a work of art. To the extent that we struggle free from pseudoidentities (i.e., those that are socially imposed and self-centered), and experience what in present-centered moments we are *truly experiencing*, remorse over the past and the postponement of life into an indefinite future are banished completely, simply by incorporating into the passing moment that unity, wholeness, balance, honesty, depth, proportion and heightened vitality that distinguish every great work of art.[9]

Clearly, the Buddhist orientation to the present is the basis for its correlation of life and art, just as the Jewish emphasis on the future is the basis for its correlation of life and ethics.

Surely, there is something very valuable in the Buddhist appreciation for the present. And when we Jews remind ourselves that "the whole earth is full of God's glory," we recognize within our own experience the wisdom expressed by the Buddhists. We recall, too, that God judged the world to be "very good," and I would suggest that it is reasonable to interpret this statement as referring to the intrinsic beauty of the world and not to its moral nature, since moral agency is usually not attributed to the natural order. Indeed, despite Judaism's concern with the future, it has avoided the temptation to become an "other-worldly" religion which totally disparages the present. While life, here and now, has been valued, however, it is less clear that the present has been *enjoyed* in a way that approximates the Buddhist enjoyment of the moment. So much of the Jewish enjoyment of life is tied to a celebration of the past — especially a remembrance of having been redeemed and chosen — and to an expectation of future events, when God's name shall be uttered by all peoples. In our attention to these other dimensions of time, the felt presence of God in every moment, in this moment, is often neglected. The Buddhist emphasis on the here-now may aid Jews in recovering a sensitivity to God's immediacy and thereby realigning the relationship between the past, present and future.

Beyond the matter of reemphasis or recovery, however, is a much larger issue that Jews may be led to consider because of their dialogue with Buddhists: the relationship between ethics and aesthetics. Within Judaism, aesthetics is understood as subordinate to or derivative from ethics. The Good is more important than the Beautiful. God does not command beauty, but goodness. A significant question raised for Judaism by the Buddhist understanding of reality is whether the Beautiful, the category of the aesthetic, is more inclusive than the Good, the category of the ethical.

In accordance with the Buddhist perspective, Charles Hartshorne has argued that since human infants and lower animals cannot fulfill ethical demands, there must be a more inclusive value. He has proposed that beauty is the universal value and that our ultimate goal should be "to make each moment contribute optimally to life in the future, one's own future so long as one survives, the future of others whom we may benefit, and above all and including all, the future of the divine life."[10] John Cobb, too, has argued for the supremacy of the aesthetic category. The ethical relationship, he notes, is a sophisticated and highly-refined process of human decision-making, yet most of life (both human and nonhuman) takes place on the unconscious level. Moreover, he contends that ethics involves judgments of things as they are; it is built on assumed knowledge and established values. Hence, "ethical action is almost always conservative." But the creative process at work in the universe cannot be fully captured in an ethical system. The system itself must be responsive to the creative urges that constitute life. What is needed, Cobb suggests, is "a spontaneity that is informed by rational ethics but transcends it."[11]

In Martin Buber's interpretation of Judaism, this revaluation of ethics is already underway. His focus on the relational "I-Thou" rather than the ethical "Thou-shalt" as central to religion clearly points beyond (and yet includes) the ethical dimension. And his emphasis on the immediacy of this relationship is consistent with the Buddhist orientation to the "now." The moral emphasis of Judaism is still ubiquitous, but it is found within a larger framework. In fact, it is the larger framework of personal relationship that both makes possible the ethical relationship and renders it resilient. At the same time, Buber's affirmation of a dimension beyond the ethical does not lead him to the repudiation of personhood. As we have seen, he is very critical of the Buddhist effort to overcome personhood and hence its inability to sustain a dialogical relationship. But Buber presents one way of integrating a characteristically Buddhist insight into a Jewish framework. His attempt to place ethics into a wider context serves as a model for how Jewish-Buddhist transformative dialogue might proceed, and thus, how it may become, for either or both traditions, the impetus for the recovery, expansion or reformation of ideas. Between Jews and Buddhists, the possibilities inherent in such dialogue are abundant. Buddhists and Jews have very different understandings of the nature of the self, salvation, time, and ultimate reality. We should explore these differences in order that we might better appreciate one another. But in addition to this, we should explore these differences out of our commitment to truth and our desire to speak it.

Conclusion

In a discussion between representatives of various faiths on the effect of the Holocaust on religious values, Irving Greenberg, the Jewish participant, writes as follows:

> Jews, Christians, and others must challenge every aspect of their traditions that overtly or covertly degrades others or nurtures hatred and thus reduces solidarity. If this means confrontation with the divine sources of the religion . . . then

this becomes the religious challenge. . . . This challenge would be testimony for God, whereas acquiescence to degradation would be testimony against God.[12]

Giving "testimony for God" even if it means confrontation with the "divine sources" is a responsibility which presses upon all religious individuals in these post-Holocaust generations. One Christian response has been the development of "theologies of continuity," which accord to Judaism a place of value that has not been superseded by Christianity. From this perspective, Judaism is viewed not as a relic of the past, but as a religion that is yet alive with value, both for itself and for other traditions. Jews too must develop a way of understanding which recognizes other traditions for their unique worth and acknowledges the possibility of their importance for Judaism. In the case of Judaism, however, it is not continuity that must be sought; continuity has been an obstacle to the appreciation of the uniqueness of non-Jewish traditions. What needs to be advanced is a "positive discontinuity" between Judaism and other traditions so that value that is independent of Judaism can be affirmed.

The reality of other traditions that are genuinely unique and truly valuable should not only be considered when the topic of interreligious relationships is raised. It must be given a central position in the development of any systematic rendering of Judaism. As David Tracy has pointed out, one consequence of dealing ex post facto with these issues has been the establishment of a "relatively external relationship to the other religions."[13] It is just such externality that frustrates the exchange of value between traditions and inhibits the zest with which religious pluralism is embraced. What Judaism is cannot be defined apart from what Judaism is in relationship with non-Jewish traditions. This is not a call for it to continue the practice of defining itself over against other religions, a practice which has left Jewish thinkers in the backwaters of self-defensiveness. It is, rather, a call to internalize the self-understanding of other traditions — as well as one can — so that they become a part of one's own self-understanding. The conscious pursuit of internal relatedness is the goal of interreligious dialogue understood to be mutually transformative, and it is a pursuit that cannot be limited only to representatives of Western traditions, but must extend to non-Western ones as well. In every case, the Jewish encounter with other traditions, understood as "testimony for God," should move in the direction of mutually transformative dialogue.

Notes

Introduction

1. Jacob B. Agus, *Dialogue and Tradition: The Challenge of Contemporary Jewish-Christian Thought* (London: Abelard-Schuman, 1971), p. v.

2. Arthur Hertzberg, "Cardinal Ratzinger Cures the Jews of an Illusion," *N.Y. Times*, Op-Ed, Section 1, p. A-23, December 22, 1987.

3. *Ibid.*, my emphasis.

4. "Veridical pluralism" is the term I have chosen to designate the position that there is very likely more than one tradition that contains some truth. The adjective "veridical" serves to distinguish this affirmation of pluralism from the affirmation of the simple fact of "cultural" pluralism. It is also intended to make it clear that this position is in opposition to philosophical relativism which often accompanies the recognition of cultural pluralism.

5. "Transformative dialogue" or "mutual transformation" are the terms used by Professor John B. Cobb, Jr., especially in his book, *Beyond Dialogue: Toward a Mutual Transformation of Christianity and Buddhism* (Philadelphia: Fortress Press, 1982) to describe the purpose and direction of dialogue in the contemporary world. In addition to outlining the assumptions and method of transformative dialogue, Cobb presents an extraordinary example of such dialogue — the culmination of years of participation in Christian-Buddhist dialogue. The ideas proposed by Professor Cobb are the framework for this present study which undertakes to apply them to the dialogue between Jews and non-Jews.

Chapter One

1. W. C. Smith and John Hick represent two approaches toward a universal theology of religion.

2. John Hick and Paul F. Knitter, eds., *The Myth of Christian Uniqueness: Toward a Pluralistic Theology of Religions* (N.Y.: Orbis Books), 1987, p. viii.

3. Langdon Gilkey, "Plurality and Its Theological Implications," in *The Myth of Christian Uniqueness*, p. 37. It is important to note that Professor Gilkey's final position is *not* relativism. He writes with great sensitivity about the "paradox of plurality," i.e., that in order to resist the demonic, we must be committed to a set of values which we

understand as ultimate, and yet, such commitment itself can become demonic. There is no intellectual way out of this paradox, but the need to act points us toward a pragmatic solution. To the either-or of absolutism and relativism, Professor Gilkey proposes a dialectic of "relative absoluteness." ". . . on the one hand, we do not relinquish our own standpoint or starting point . . . Nor on the other hand do we absolutize our own standpoint. . . . On the contrary, we relativize it radically: truth and grace are *also* with the other, so that now ours is only *one* way. And yet we remain *there*: embodying stubbornly but relatively our unconditional affirmations" [p. 47].

4. *Ibid.*, p. 44.

5. David Hartman, *The Breakdown of Tradition and the Quest for Renewal* (Jerusalem: The Gate Press), 1980, p. 33.

6. *Ibid.*

7. In this book I do not emphasize the extraordinary nature of the Noachide framework provided for by traditional Judaism. Indeed, I am critical of the notion because I believe it to be an anachronistic way for Jews to map out a relationship with non-Jews in the late twentieth century. However, the notion that people of another faith are not necessarily excluded from salvation, providing that they abide by the Noachide covenant, is historically an exceedingly liberal and progressive notion. It is an idea that was formulated early on in Judaism, sometime during the first century C.E.. In contrast to this Jewish framework, we have the inglorious words of Pope Gregory XVI, written within the last century and a half.

We come now to a source which is, alas! all too productive of the deplorable evils afflicting the Church today. We have in mind indifferentism, that is, the fatal opinion everywhere spread abroad by the deceit of wicked men, that the eternal salvation of the soul can be won by the profession of any faith at all, provided that conduct conforms to the norms of justice and probity. (Quoted by Leonard Swidler in *Toward a Universal Theology of Religion* [New York: Orbis Books], 1987, p. 6.)

8. John B. Cobb, Jr., *Beyond Dialogue: Toward a Mutual Transformation of Christianity and Buddhism* (Philadelphia: Fortress Press), 1982.

9. *Ibid.*, p. 47, my emphasis.

10. I am grateful to Gary Bollinger who articulates these assumptions so well in his dissertation, *Personal Faith and Interfaith Encounter*, Claremont Graduate School, 1981.

11. Eugene B. Borowitz, "A Jewish Response: The Lure and Limits of Universalizing our Faith," in Donald G. Dawe and John B. Carman, eds., *Christian Faith in a Religiously Plural World* (New York: Orbis Books, 1978), p. 67.

12. *Ibid.*, p. 62.

13. Cobb, *Beyond Dialogue*, p. 46.

14. Charles Birch and John B. Cobb, Jr., *Liberation of Life: From the Cell to the Community* (Cambridge: Cambridge University Press), 1985, p. 187.

15. John B. Cobb, Jr., "The Meaning of Pluralism for Christian Self-Understanding," in Leroy S. Rouner, ed., *Religious Pluralism* (University of Notre Dame Press), 1984, p. 172.

16. Cobb's position on transformative dialogue has been criticized. There are two main camps of such criticism: there are those who believe that such dialogue should not take place and those who believe that it is not possible.

In the first camp are those who oppose any affirmation of pluralism that does not stoutly affirm Christianity as the final and absolute form of religion. The supremacy of the Christian faith above all other faiths is fundamental to their understanding of Christianity per se. Any solution to the "problem" of many faiths that dethrones classical Christian notions, especially the notion of superiority, is rejected on the grounds that Christianity simply cannot properly be thought of in this way.

This same camp includes many who are no longer fully comfortable with assertions of Christian superiority, yet who maintain that Cobb's approach to dialogue, along with that of John Hick, Paul Knitter, and Wilfred Cantwell Smith, is dangerous. Characterized as "radical attempts to departicularize Christian faith," the assumption is that such dialogue will result in a relativizing of Christian identity. (Gabriel Fackre, reviewing Cobb's book, *Beyond Dialogue, International Bulletin of Missionary Research*, Jan., 1984, p. 42.) In short, pluralism is regarded as simply another avenue to relativism.

I have argued in this essay, as have Cobb, Hick, Smith, Knitter, and others elsewhere, that pluralism is something other than relativism. But even among those who affirm pluralism as a third option, there are disagreements. Whereas John Hick and W. C. Smith are impressive proponents of dialogue, they are not advocates of "transformative" dialogue. In brief, Hick and Smith believe that all religions are, at heart, the same. Encounter between faiths will yield a better understanding of their essential likenesses, but it will not yield transformation, simply because likeness is no impulse for transformation. Thus, in this view, dialogue is not an encounter with the "other;" rather, it is an encounter with one's own selfhood, differently expressed. And dialogue should be undertaken because it leads to a greater understanding of the one truth that unifies us all; as such, it leads to peace. It does not, however, open us up to new truths; hence, transformation of the sort advocated by Cobb is not possible.

Cobb rejects the assumption that all religions are fundamentally concerned with the same thing — for example, what Hick calls the "transcendent ground of all existence, including personal existence." (John Hick, "Toward a Philosophy of Religious Pluralism," *Neue Zeitschrift für systematische Theologie*, 22 [1980]:145) Mahayana Buddhists, Cobb argues, are *not* engaged in a unique form of worshiping God; *Sunyata* is not what Christians, Jews, and Muslims identify as God.

> The Buddhist might propose that what all religions are truly concerned with is Emptiness or the absolutely immanent process of dependent origination. But it is significant that Emptiness is not an object of worship for Buddhists, whereas there can be little doubt that worship is, for Hick, central to his concerns. . . . Given this situation it is not illuminating to insist that Emptiness and God are two names for the same noumenal reality. Unless something in the character of the experience warrants that judgment, it is arbitrary, and at the present time the evidence counts in favor of a different hypothesis. If one continues to insist that Buddhist Emptiness is God despite Buddhist objections, the problem that arises is similar to that raised by calling Buddhists anonymous Christians. [Cobb, *Beyond Dialogue*, p. 43]

Cobb's hypothesis is this:

> [W]here worship is felt to be the appropriate response to religious experience . . .
> something like what Hick calls God is the reality experienced. . . . [W]here
> meditation directed toward the realization of what one truly is is the appropriate
> activity, something like what the Buddhists call Emptiness is the reality that is
> realized. [Cobb, *Beyond Dialogue*, p. 44]

It is Cobb's hypothesis, based on his encounter with Buddhism, that makes transformative dialogue not only possible, but necessary.

Cobb's rejection of the notion that religions have a common essence has led, at least
in one instance, to the erroneous assessment that he also rejects the position that there
is an objective reality within which truth coheres. Paul Knitter argues that Cobb's
denial of a "universal theory" or "common source" of religion and his simultaneous call
for transformative dialogue creates a paradox, the paradox of holding that "incommensurable traditions can indeed communicate with one another." (Paul Knitter, "Toward
a Liberation Theology of Religions," in John Hick and Paul F. Knitter, eds., *The Myth
of Christian Uniqueness* [New York: Orbis Books, 1987], p. 184.) Knitter makes no
distinction between Cobb's approach and that of Richard Bernstein, who argues for a
position "beyond objectivism." (Richard Bernstein, *Beyond Objectivism and Relativism:
Science, Hermeneutics, and Praxis* [Philadelphia, University of Pennsylvania Press, 1983.])
"Incommensurability" in any metaphysical sense is not, however, Cobb's starting
point. He writes:

> As a Christian I find that I do recognize that there are truths that have been
> discovered by others, through their special meditative techniques or their unique
> historical experience, which I have not learned in my tradition. I see also that
> the systems of thought that center on these different truths do conflict with the
> system of thought that I bring with me to the dialogue. *But it is my deepest
> conviction that no truth contradicts any other truth. In this respect I am, I suppose, a
> rationalist, and I do not see how a Christian can be anything else.* (John B. Cobb, Jr.,
> "Response to Wiebe," in *Buddhist-Christian Studies* 6[1986]:151, my emphasis.)

If there is truth to the Buddhist vision of reality, then it must cohere with whatever
truth lies within the Christian vision of reality. Truths can never be incommensurable.
Our task in dialogue is not to assume commonalities, but to find the truths that sustain
the religions of the world.

Finally, there are those who argue that transformative dialogue is psychologically
impossible. This criticism is rooted in the assumption that it is not possible to "pass
over" into another tradition and experience "the other" without losing "one's self." Such
a criticism presupposes a substantialist view of the self which, in regard to dialogue,
sets up the dichotomy of conversion or rejection as the only responses to interreligious
encounter. Insofar as transformation, as Cobb describes it, entails a "coming back," it
is very different from conversion; insofar as it means "coming back *changed*," it is very
different from rejection. Almost everyone today agrees that it *is* possible to cross over,
that is, to convert. So the debate lies in whether it is possible to "come back" without

entirely rejecting what one has encountered in the other faith. It seems that anyone who has experienced a relationship of love knows that it is possible to "know" another in such a way that one's own "selfhood" is both transcended and fulfilled. If all goes well in love, one never disengages oneself from the other, and yet a healthy relationship demands that one does not simply become the other either. The example of a relationship of love is fully appropriate to the topic of dialogue. For dialogue is nothing other than a relationship of love — love for the other and for one's own tradition, love for the world and love for God.

Chapter Two

1. David Novak, *The Image of the Non-Jew in Judaism, An Historical and Constructive Study of the Noachide Laws*, Toronto Studies in Theology, vol. 14 (New York and Toronto: Edwin Mellon Press, 1983), p. xiii.

2. David Novak, "The Origin of the Noachide Laws," in Arthur A. Chiel, ed., *Perspectives on Jews and Judaism: Essays in Honor of Wolfe Kelman* (New York: The Rabbinical Assembly, 1978), p. 309.

3. Given in Talmud (B. T. *Sanh.* 56a-60a, *Tosefta Avodah Zarah*, 8:4-8), based on Gen. 9:1-17.

4. Clearly, non-Jews who adhere to their own religious traditions find the Noachide laws lacking in salvific, cognitive, and symbolic power.

5. Elijah Benamozegh, quoted in Samuel Hugo Bergman, "Israel and the Oikoumene," in Raphael Lowe, ed., *Studies in Rationalism, Judaism, and Universalism* (London: Routledge and Kegan Paul, 1966), pp. 53-54, my emphasis.

6. For the following discussion on medieval and enlightenment attitudes of Jews toward non-Jews I have relied heavily on Jacob Katz, *Exclusiveness and Tolerance: Jewish-Gentile Relations in Medieval and Modern Times* (New York: Schocken Books, 1962).

7. Katz, *Exclusiveness and Tolerance*, p. 24.

8. Katz, pp. 24, 162 and elsewhere. Katz makes a clear distinction between the doctrinal level, at which Christianity was not differentiated from other forms of idolatry, and the practical level of economic and social intercourse, at which Christianity was exempted from the category of idolatry (pp. 24-36). It is on the practical level only that the Christian notion of the trinity is designated "*shittuf,*" literally "partnership," and not considered to be a form of idolatry for Christians, although it remains so for Jews. The Jewish tolerance of Christians in the Middle Ages was based on pragmatic concerns and not on theological principle. Because H. J. Schoeps (*The Jewish-Christian Argument, A History of Theologies in Conflict*, trans. David E. Green [New York: Holt, Rinehart and Winston, 1963], pp. 14-15) in his discussion of Christianity as "shittuf" does not make this distinction, he reaches the conclusion that there was a greater degree of tolerance.

9. Moses Maimonides, "Epistle to Yemen," in Isadore Twersky, ed., *A Maimonides Reader* (New York: Behrman House, Inc., 1972), p. 442.

10. Although at the close of his *Mishneh Torah* Maimonides gives some positive bearing to Christianity and Islam — as "preparations" for the Messiah, making the "uncircumcised of heart and flesh" familiar with the "Messianic hope, the Torah, and the commandments," (*A Reader*, pp. 226-27) — I believe H. J. Schoeps is correct when

he asserts that this should be treated as an "occasional speculation" and not as a significant breakthrough in medieval thought. "In the last analysis, Christians and Moslems were viewed as people who had strayed from the truth" (*Christian-Jewish Argument*, p. 76).

11. The standard position as expressed by Rashi was, "Although he has sinned, he remains a Jew." Quoted in Katz, *Exclusiveness and Tolerance*, p. 71.

12. Katz, *Exclusiveness and Tolerance*, p. 24.

13. *Ibid.*

14. *Ibid.*, pp. 121, 120.

15. R. Jacob Emden, "Seder Olam" (from a letter written in 1757), quoted in Schoeps, *Jewish-Christian Argument*, p. 192.

16. Moses Mendelssohn, *Jerusalem and Other Jewish Writings*, trans. and ed. Alfred Jospe (New York: Schocken Books, 1969), pp. 128, 117.

17. *Ibid.*, pp. 134, 137.

18. *Ibid.*, pp. 116–117, my emphasis.

19. *Ibid.*, p. 129. For Mendelssohn it is not necessary that the non-Jew believe the Noachide laws to have been divinely revealed. For Maimonides, natural religion was idolatrous, whereas Mendelssohn finds natural religion to be the essence or internal element of revealed religion.

20. *Ibid.*, p. 123.

21. Jochanan H. A. Wijnhoven, "Convert and Conversion," in Arthur A. Cohen and Paul Mendes-Flohr, eds., *Contemporary Jewish Religious Thought* (N.Y.: Charles Scribner's, 1987), p. 104.

22. Walter Jacob, *Christianity Through Jewish Eyes: The Quest for Common Ground* (Hebrew Union College Press, 1974), p. 54.

23. *Ibid.*, p. 58.

24. *Ibid.*, p. 47.

25. *Ibid.*, p. 89.

26. *Ibid.*, p. 91.

27. "Bibliographical Essay: Judaism on Christianity: Christianity on Judaism," in F. E. Talmage, ed., *Disputation and Dialogue: Readings in the Jewish-Christian Encounter* (New York: KTAV Publishing House, 1975), p. 368. He continues this passage by adding, "This trend reached a turning point of sorts in the writings of Franz Rosenzweig."

28. Gershom Scholem, *On Jews and Judaism in Crisis: Selected Essays*, ed. Werner J. Dannhauser (New York, Schocken Books, 1976), p. 87.

29. Jacob, *Christianity Through Jewish Eyes*, pp. 5–6.

30. Scholem, *On Jews and Judaism in Crisis*, pp. 86–90.

Chapter Three

1. Leo Baeck, "Some Questions to the Christian Church from the Jewish Point of View," in Gote Hedenquist, ed., *The Church and the Jewish People* (London: Edinburgh House Press, 1954), p. 103.

2. *Ibid.*, p. 104, my emphasis.

3. *Ibid.*

4. *Ibid.*, pp. 105, 108, 111, 115.

5. *Ibid.*, pp. 113, 114.

6. *Ibid.*, p. 109.

7. *Ibid.*, p. 116.

8. Leo Baeck, "Types of Jewish Understanding from Moses Mendelssohn to Franz Rosenzweig," *Judaism* 9(1960):9.

9. It is striking that in this lecture Baeck offers an interpretation of Mendelssohn's "solution" to the call of universalism and the demands of religious particularism that is *Baeck's* answer. Baeck does not make clear the difference between what he means by the revelation at Sinai and what Mendelssohn means, a quite significant blurring.

Mendelssohn wrote that in the fundamentals of its faith, the Jewish religion is essentially a religion of reason, amenable to and justifiable by reason, and yet truly to be considered as religion. But within this religion, there is the task that a people . . . was faced with at Sinai: a task was committed to that people, to be true to itself, so that through Revelation they came to personify Truth, down to the end of historical time. Nothing rational can explain that. The fact, however, remains, the fact of this people as a bearer of revelation. And therefore, so Mendelssohn now said — and thus provided the answer that was to be given — the Jew must be a man of reason, yet entirely a Jew, completely retaining his individuality, yet living in his tradition, without which there is no history. ["Types of Jewish Understanding," p. 9]

10. Leo Baeck, *The Essence of Judaism* (1948) (New York: Schocken Paperback, 1961), p. 59.

11. Leo Baeck, quoted in Albert H. Friedlander, *Leo Baeck, Teacher of Theriesienstadt* (New York: Holt, Rinehart, and Winston, 1968), p. 318.

12. Baeck, *Essence*, p. 56.

13. *Ibid.*, p. 37.

14. Leo Baeck, *This People Israel: The Meaning of Jewish Existence*, translated and with an introductory essay by Albert H. Friedlander (New York: Holt, Rinehart and Winston, 1965), p. 23.

15. Leo Baeck, *God and Man in Judaism* (New York: Union of American Hebrew Congregations, 1958), pp. 24, 9, 23, my emphasis.

16. Deut. 10:19, quoted in Baeck, *Essence*, p. 40.

17. It is for this general reduction of religion to ethics, and of Judaism in particular to ethics, that Baeck is often criticized by other Jewish thinkers. See for example, Arthur Cohen, *The Natural and the Supernatural Jew* (New York: Panthenon, 1962), pp. 102-120; Alexander Altmann, "Theology in Twentieth Century German Jewry," *Leo Baeck Institute Year Book I* (London, 1956), p. 200.

18. Baeck, *Essence*, p. 36.

19. Baeck, *This People*, p. 25.

20. Baeck, *Essence*, p. 25.

21. *Ibid.*, p. 35.

22. Leo Baeck, "Why Jews in the World? A Reaffirmation of Faith in Israel's Destiny," *Commentary*, 3(1946):503.

23. Leo Baeck, "Theology and History," trans. Michael A. Meyer, *Judaism*, 13(1964):281.

24. Leo Baeck, "Romantic Religion," in *Judaism and Christianity: Essays by Leo Baeck*, trans. Walter Kaufmann (New York: Atheneum, 1970), p. 171.

25. Friedlander, *Leo Baeck*, p. 159.

26. *Ibid.*, pp. 141–204.

27. Baeck, "Theology and History," p. 282.

28. Baeck, *Essence*, p. 56.

29. *Ibid.*, p. 194.

30. *Ibid.*, p. 10.

31. Baeck, "Some Questions," p. 104.

32. Baeck, *Essence*, p. 198.

33. Baeck, *This People*, p. 318, my emphasis.

34. Friedlander, *Leo Baeck*, p. 15.

35. Baeck, *Essence*, p. 198.

36. Baeck, *Judaism and Christianity*, p. 229.

37. Baeck, *This People*, p. 20.

38. Leo Baeck, "Does Traditional Judaism Possess Dogmas?" in Alfred Jospe, ed., *Studies in Jewish Thought: An Anthology of German Jewish Scholarship* (Detroit: Wayne State University Press, 1981), p. 47.

39. *Ibid.*, pp. 46, 47. Baeck contends that even the Sanhedrin could not establish "irrefutable religious doctrines" (p. 47).

40. See, for example, Max Gruenwald, "Leo Baeck: Witness and Judge," *Judaism*, 6(1957):200.

41. Baeck, "Does Traditional Judaism Possess Dogmas?" p. 49.

42. *Ibid.*, pp. 49–50.

43. *Ibid.*, p. 49.

44. *Ibid.*

45. Baeck, *Essence*, p. 35.

46. *Ibid.*, p. 43.

47. *Ibid.*

48. *Ibid.*, p. 25.

49. Baeck, *This People Israel*, p. 25.

50. Baeck, *Essence*, p. 60.

51. *Ibid.*, pp. 60–61.

52. Baeck's comparison of Judaism and Buddhism is a good example of what Walter Kaufmann calls Baeck's idiom, "Es ist ein zweifachs" — "It is something twofold." Kaufmann writes, "He discusses [the two-fold concepts] as if they were entities: he explains them not functionally but antithetically by placing them off against some counter concept. We see it again most clearly in his discussion of Romantic and Classical religions" (Kaufmann's introduction to Baeck's *Judaism and Christianity*, p. 8.)

53. Baeck, *Essence*, p. 61.

54. Baeck, "Romantic Religion," *Judaism and Christianity*, p. 198.

55. *Ibid.*, p. 101, my emphasis; p. 102.

56. *Ibid.*, p. 211.

57. Leo Baeck, *The Pharisees and Other Essays* (New York: Schocken Books, 1947), pp. 82, 89, 90.

58. *Ibid.*, pp. 90, 82.

59. Baeck, *This People Israel*, p. 12.

60. *Ibid.*, p. 20.

61. Gen. 9:9, quoted in Baeck, *This People Israel*, p. 17.

62. *Ibid.*, p. 9.

63. Exod. 19:5-6, quoted in Baeck, *This People Israel*, p. 18, my emphasis.

64. Eugene Borowitz summarizes Baeck's strategy precisely: "What ethical theory had made improbable, the coordinate theory of religious consciousness has now explained." *Choices in Modern Jewish Thought* (New York: Behrman House, Inc. 1983), p. 67.

65. Baeck, *This People Israel*, p. 21, my emphasis.

66. *Ibid.*, p. 26.

67. Baeck, *God and Man in Judaism*, p. 66.

68. Baeck, *This People Israel*, p. 26.

69. Baeck, "Theology and History," pp. 281, 275, 281, my emphasis.

70. *Ibid.*, p. 282.

71. Baeck, *Essence*, p. 29.

72. Baeck, "Theology and History," p. 282.

73. Baeck, *The Pharisees*, p. 149.

74. Isa. 59:21.

75. Baeck, *God and Man*, pp. 18, 14, my emphasis.

76. Baeck, *Essence*, p. 48.

77. *Ibid.*, p. 275.

78. Baeck, *This People Israel*, p. 318.

79. Indeed, for Baeck, the intense individuality of those who make up the people of Israel is tempered by their participation in the community — for example, when he speaks of the covenant as something that cannot be forsaken by the generations.

Chapter Four

1. Franz Rosenzweig, *Understanding the Sick and the Healthy* (New York: The Noonday Press, 1974), p. 123.

2. Rosenzweig, quoted in Walter Jacob, *Christianity Through Jewish Eyes: The Quest for Common Ground* (Hebrew Union College Press, 1974), p. 123.

3. Indeed, Rosenzweig's differences with Baeck run very deep. Rosenzweig rejects the kind of Judaism which defines its essence as ethical monotheism. Rosenzweig believes that religion is fundamentally concerned with the relationship between the individual and God, and while that relationship leads to an ethical relationship between the individual and those who are encountered, the basis of religion is not ethics but revelation. "Ethics has its origin outside religion, in the intercourse between men, and is only brought into the domain of religion in order to support it." (Rosenzweig, quoted in Nahum N. Glatzer, *Franz Rosenzweig: His Life and Thought* [New York: Schocken Books, 1953; second and revised ed. 1961], p. 8.)

4. Alexander Altmann, "Franz Rosenzweig and Eugen Rosenstock-Huessy: An Introduction to Their Letters on Judaism and Christianity," in Eugen Rosenstock-Huessy, ed. *Judaism Despite Christianity* (University, Alabama: University of Alabama Press, 1969), p. 27.

5. Rosenstock-Huessy, *Judaism Despite Christianity*, p. 176. Hereafter cited as *JDC*.

6. Rosenzweig, *Understanding the Sick and Healthy*, p. 47.

7. Rosenzweig, quoted in Nahum N. Glatzer, *Franz Rosenzweig: His Life and Thought* (New York: Schocken Books, 1953; Second, revised ed., 1961), p. 200. Hereafter cited as *Life and Thought*.

8. Rosenzweig, *Understanding the Sick and Healthy*, pp. 69, 68.

9. *Ibid.*, p. 90.

10. Rosenzweig, quoted in Glatzer, *Life and Thought*, pp. 180, 183.

11. *Ibid.*, p. 90.

12. *Ibid.*, p. 205.

13. Rosenzweig, *Understanding the Sick and Healthy*, p. 61.

14. Rosenzweig, quoted in Glatzer, *Life and Thought*, pp. 193, 198.

15. *Ibid.*, p. 199, my emphasis.

16. Rosenzweig, *Understanding the Sick and Healthy*, p. 69.

17. Rosenzweig, quoted in Glatzer, *Life and Thought*, p. 199.

18. Rosenzweig in Rosenstock-Huessy, *JDC*, p. 167.

19. Franz Rosenzweig, *The Star of Redemption* (1930), trans. William W. Hallo (Boston: Beacon Press, 1972), p. 33.

20. Rosenzweig, quoted in Jacob, *Christianity Through Jewish Eyes*, pp. 123–124.

21. Rosenzweig, quoted in Glatzer, *Life and Thought*, p. 195.

22. *Ibid.*, p. 202.

23. Rosenzweig, *Star*, p. 37.

24. Rosenzweig, quoted in Glatzer, *Life and Thought*, p. 203.

25. Rosenzweig in Rosenstock-Huessy, *JDC*, p. 165.

26. Rosenzweig, *Star*, pp. 117, 216.

27. Rosenzweig, quoted in Glatzer, *Life and Thought*, p. 202.

28. Rosenzweig in Rosenstock-Huessy, *JDC*, p. 165.

29. *Ibid.*, p. 164.

30. *Ibid.*, p. 146.

31. *Ibid.*, p. 134.

32. Rosenzweig, quoted in Glatzer, *Life and Thought*, p. 9.

33. *Ibid.*, pp. 8–9.

34. *Ibid.*, p. 19.

35. Rosenzweig in Rosenstock-Huessy, *JDC*, p. 113.

36. Rosenzweig, quoted in Glatzer, *Life and Thought*, p. 206.

37. *Ibid.*, p. xxxii.

38. *Ibid.*, p. 204.

39. Rosenzweig, *Star*, p. 331, my emphasis.

40. In the Sabbath morning service Rosenzweig notes, ". . . we find utterances of the people's awareness of being elect through the gift of Torah which signifies that eternal life has been planted in their midst." (Rosenzweig, in Glatzer, *Life and Thought*, p. 312).

41. Rosenzweig in Rosenstock-Huessy, *JDC*, p. 160.

42. Rosenzweig, quoted in Alexander Altmann, "Franz Rosenzweig on History," in *Between East* and *West* (London, 1958), p. 208. See also pp. 208–210.

43. Rosenzweig, *Star*, p. 328.

44. *Ibid.*, p. 179.

45. *Ibid.*, pp. 298–299.

46. Rosenzweig in Rosenstock-Huessy, *JDC*, p. 115.

47. Rosenzweig, quoted in Glatzer, *Life and Thought*, p. 73.

48. Rosenzweig's characterization of Judaism as ahistorical is in direct contrast to Baeck's understanding of Judaism; indeed the "ahistorical" nature of Christianity is fundamental to Baeck's criticism of it as "romantic" religion.

49. Rosenzweig, *Star*, p. 304.

50. *Ibid.*, p. 298.

51. *Ibid.*, p. 355.

52. *Ibid.*, p. 305.

53. *Ibid.*

54. Rosenzweig in Rosenstock-Huessy, *JDC*, p. 113.

55. Poul Borchsenius, quoted in Maurice G. Bowler, "Rosenzweig on Judaism and Christianity—The Two Covenant Theory," *Judaism* , 22(1973):476. Also in this regard see M. Bowler, "The Reconcilation of Church and Synagogue in Franz Rosenzweig" (Master's thesis, Sir George Williams University, 1972), pp. 57–87. I concur with Bowler that Rosenzweig places important limitations on the validity of Christianity, limitations which function to make Christianity appear to be dependent on and significantly inferior to Judaism.

56. Rosenzweig, quoted in Glatzer, *Life and Thought*, p. 203.

57. *Ibid.*, p. 203.

58. *Ibid.*, pp. 204, 207.

59. *Ibid.*, p. 206.

60. Rosenzweig, *Star*, p. 393.

61. Rosenzweig, quoted in Glatzer, *Life and Thought*, pp. 206, 207.

62. *Ibid.*, pp. 206–207.

63. Rosenzweig, *Star*, p. 379. See Judah Halevi, *The Kuzari: An Argument for the Faith of Israel*, Intro. by Henry Slonimsky (New York: Schocken Books, 1964), pp. 226–227.

64. *Ibid.*, my emphasis.

65. Rosenzweig, *Star*, p. 415.

66. *Ibid.*

67. *Ibid.*, p. 378.

68. *Ibid.*, p. 407.

69. *Ibid.*, p. 397.

70. Rosenzweig in Rosenstock-Huessy, *JDC*, p. 131.

71. Rosenzweig, *Star*, p. 350, my emphasis.

72. *Ibid.*, p. 413.

73. Rosenzweig in Rosenstock-Huessy, *JDC*, p. 130.

74. Rosenzweig, *Star*, pp. 407, 415.

75. *Ibid.*, p. 416, my emphasis.

76. *Ibid.*, pp. 331, 335, 332.

77. *Ibid.*, p. 408.

78. Rosenzweig in Rosenstock-Huessy, *JDC*, p. 136.

79. Arthur A. Cohen, *The Natural and the Supernatural Jew* (New York: Behrman House, Inc., 1979) pp. 141–143.

80. Rosenzweig, *Star*, p. 335.

81. *Ibid.*

82. *Ibid.*, p. 423.

83. Rosenzweig, quoted in Glatzer, *Life and Thought*, p. 107.

84. *Ibid.*, p. 31.

85. Alfred North Whitehead, *Process and Reality*, corrected edition, ed. David Ray Griffin and Donald W. Sherburne (New York: The Free Press, 1978), p. 348.

86. Rosenzweig, quoted in Glatzer, *Life and Thought*, p. 205.

87. *Ibid.*, pp. 285, xxxii.

Chapter Five

1. Martin Buber, *The Philosophy of Martin Buber*, ed. Paul Arthur Schilpp and Maurice Friedman, *The Library of Living Philosophers*, vol. 12 (La Salle, Ill.: Open Court Publishing Company, 1967), p. 8.

2. *Ibid.*

3. Martin Buber, *Israel and the World: Essays in a Time of Crisis*, 2nd ed. (New York: Schocken Books, 1963), p. 40.

4. Martin Buber, *Pointing the Way*, ed. and trans. Maurice Friedman (New York: Harper Torchbooks, 1963), pp. 234–235.

5. Martin Buber, *For the Sake of Heaven* (New York: Meridian Books—Jewish Publication Society, 1958), p. xiii.

6. See for example, Malcolm Diamond, *Martin Buber: Jewish Existentialist* (New York: Oxford University Press, 1960), p. 190 and Ernst Simon, "The Builder of Bridges," trans. David Wolf Silverman, *Judaism*, 27(1978):157.

7. Martin Buber, *I and Thou*, 2nd ed., trans. R. G. Smith (New York: Charles Scribner's Sons, 1958), p. 60.

8. *Ibid.*, p. 62.

9. Martin Buber, *The Knowledge of Man, A Philosophy of the Interhuman*, ed. M. Friedman, trans. M. Friedman and R. G. Smith (New York: Harper Torchbooks, 1966), p. 112.

10. *Ibid.*, p. 75.

11. Martin Buber, *Between Man and Man*, trans. R. G. Smith (New York: The MacMillan Company, 1948), p. 203.

12. Buber, *Knowledge of Man*, pp. 60, 62.

13. *Ibid.*, p. 64.

14. *Ibid.*, pp. 68, 69, 71.

15. Buber, *I and Thou*, p. 113.

16. Buber, *Knowledge of Man*, pp. 80, 70.

17. *Ibid.*, p. 70.

18. *Ibid.*, p. 71.

19. Buber, *Knowledge of Man*, pp. 113, 78.

20. Buber, *Between Man and Man*, pp. 19–29.

21. Buber, *Knowledge of Man*, p. 113.

22. *Ibid.*, p. 77; Buber, *Between Man and Man*, p. 36.

23. Buber, *I and Thou*, p. 115.

24. Buber, *Knowledge of Man*, p. 113.

25. Buber, *I and Thou*, pp. 82, 58.

26. *Ibid.*, pp. 58, 66.

27. Buber, *Between Man and Man*, p. 170.

28. Buber, *Knowledge of Man*, p. 69, my emphasis.

29. *Ibid.*, p. 114.

30. *Ibid.*, p. 77.

31. Maurice S. Friedman, *Martin Buber, The Life of Dialogue* (Chicago: University of Chicago Press, 1955), p. 164. Friedman is quoting the German theologian, Karl Heim.

32. Buber, *I and Thou*, p. 62.

33. Emmanuel Levinas, "Martin Buber and the Theory of Knowledge," in Schilpp, *The Philosophy of Martin Buber*, p. 143, quoting Buber, *Dialogisches Leben*, p. 283.

34. Buber, *I and Thou*, pp. 69, 89.

35. Buber, *Between Man and Man*, p. 12.

36. Buber, *I and Thou*, p. 158.

37. Martin Buber, *Eclipse of God: Studies in the Relation Between Religion and Philosophy* (New York: Harper and Row, 1952), pp. 44–45.

38. Buber, *I and Thou*, pp. 112, 159, 160.

39. Buber, *Between Man and Man*, p. 15.

40. *Ibid.*, p. 7, my emphasis.

41. *Ibid.*, pp. 17–18.

42. Buber, *I and Thou*, p. 62.

43. Buber, *Between Man and Man*, p. 52.

44. Martin Buber, *On Judaism* (New York: Schocken Books, 1967), pp. 11–12.

45. Robert Welch, quoted by Pinchas H. Peli, " 'Jewish Religiosity' According to Buber," *Immanuel* 13(1981):109. Many others echoed this evaluation—for example, Gershom Scholem and Hugo Bergman. Since many of those who heard Buber's addresses later became leaders in Jewish thought, e.g., Ernst Simon, Max Brod, Scholem, Bergman, Franz Kafka, the importance of these speeches is hard to overestimate.

46. Buber, *On Judaism*, pp. 79, 13, 80.

Buber does not use the basic word "I-Thou" in these early lectures. That language which so fully expresses his thought is not spoken by Buber until more than a decade after his lectures, *On Judaism*. Chronologically, then, it is misleading to use this terminology here. However, my task is not to chronicle the development of Buber's thought, but rather to capture the essence of it. Virtually all major Buber scholars agree that while Buber refines his ideas and the expression of his ideas throughout his long life, his "fundamental vision" remains steady.

It is Pinchas Peli who uses the language of "fundamental vision" to describe the connectedness between Buber's early lectures on "Jewish Religiosity" and the tasks that occupied him throughout his career. That speech, Peli argues, "in certain respects . . .

anticipates and invites these later works (i.e., *I and Thou* and Buber's studies of Hasidism and the Bible)." (Pinchas Ha-Cohen Peli, " 'Jewish Religiosity' According to Buber," in Haim Gordon and Jochanan Bloch, eds., *Martin Buber, A Centenary Volume* [New York: KTAV, 1984], p. 419.) Maurice Friedman talks about Buber's thought as moving from "immature" to "mature" expression, wherein the mature is not a rejection of the former ideas but a clarification and deepening of them. (*Martin Buber's Life and Work: The Early Years, 1878–1923*, N.Y.: E. P. Dutton, 1981.) Gershom Scholem, too, in his excellent summary essay on Buber's thought, argues that although "there are two periods in Buber's preoccupation with Judaism that correspond to his efforts as a thinker in general," there is a core that is common to them. "Throughout . . . the key word in which his thinking is summed up remains 'realization' (*Verwirklichung*), though the way to the latter is now substantiated in another matter." (*On Jews and Judaism in Crisis*, [New York: Schocken Books, 1976], pp. 147–148.) Scholem acknowledges the shifts in Buber's thought from his early essays to his later ones, and he makes clear Buber's own assessment that his position had at times changed dramatically. Nonetheless, the principle that informs Buber's work on Judaism remains the same — differently articulated and differently illuminated over the years. This central principle might be rendered in shorthand as "religiosity," and in its most enlightening form as "the unmediated relation of I and Thou."

47. Buber, *Israel and the World*, p. 19.

48. Buber, *On Judaism*, pp. 80, 81, 80.

49. Martin Buber, *Two Types of Faith (A Study in the Interpenetration of Judaism and Christianity)* (New York: Harper Torchbooks, 1961), pp. 26, 154.

50. Buber, *On Judaism*, p. 54.

51. *Ibid.*, p. 40.

52. *Ibid.*, pp. 29, 25, 33.

53. *Ibid.*, p. 81.

54. *Ibid.*, p. 12.

55. Buber, *Israel and the World*, p. 16.

56. Martin Buber, *Kingship of God*, trans. Richard Scheimann (New York: Harper and Row, 1967), p. 119.

57. *Ibid.*, p. 126.

58. *Ibid.*, p. 109.

59. Buber, *Israel and the World*, p. 170.

60. Buber, *Kingship of God*, p. 109.

61. Buber, *Israel and the World*, p. 170.

62. Martin Buber, "Church, State, Nation, Jewry," in David W. McKain, ed., *Christianity: Some Non-Christian Appraisals* (New York: McGraw-Hill, 1964), pp. 182–183.

63. Buber, *On Judaism*, pp. 13, 9.

64. *Ibid.*, pp. 20, 15–16; pp. 75–76, my emphasis.

65. Steven Schwarzschild, in his article, "Martin Buber's Zionism," *Jewish Peace Fellowship Tidings*, September 1947, p. 4, places Buber's racialism in some perspective.

Buber's concept of national self-consciousness is difficult to understand and to sympathize with for anyone not familiar with certain mystical traditions and with the strain of vitalism in modern thought which was expressed by such men as Nietzsche and Carl Jung.

66. Hans Urs von Balthasar, "Martin Buber and Christianity," in Paul A. Schilpp and Maurice Friedman, eds., *The Philosophy of Martin Buber*, pp. 341–359. See also Maurice Friedman, *Martin Buber's Life and Work: The Later Yeas, 1945–1965* (New York: E. P. Dutton, 1983), pp. 90–101.

67. Buber, "Church, State, Nation, Jewry," p. 181.

68. Buber, *Two Types*, pp. 8, 72.

69. Buber, *Between Man and Man*, p. 5.

70. Buber, *Two Types*, pp. 12–13.

71. Martin Buber, *The Origin and Meaning of Hasidism*, ed. and trans. Maurice Friedman (New York: Harper Torchbooks, 1966), p. 109.

72. *Ibid.*

73. *Ibid.*, p. 86.

74. *Ibid.*, p. 251.

75. *Ibid.*, p. 111.

76. *Ibid.*, p. 74.

77. *Ibid.*, p. 244.

78. *Ibid.*, p. 247.

79. *Ibid.*, p. 251.

80. Buber, *On Judaism*, p. 70.

81. Buber, *Origin and Meaning*, p. 66, my emphasis.

82. Buber, *On Judaism*, pp. 45, 47.

83. *Ibid.*, pp. 46–47. On page 45 Buber writes: "Whatever was not eclectic, whatever was creative in the beginnings of Christianity, was nothing but Judaism." And again on page 70: "But what remained enduringly creative in Christianity had originally been Judaism's prime possession."

84. Buber, *Two Types*, p. 75. Buber adds the following important note: "But one should not fail to appreciate the bearers of the plain light below from amongst whom he arose, those who enjoined much that was possible so as not to cause men to despair of being able to serve God in their poor everyday affairs."

85. Buber, *For the Sake of Heaven*, p. xii.

86. Buber, *Two Types*, p. 132.

87. *Ibid.*, pp. 131, 130.

88. *Ibid.*, pp. 133, 130. "The One Who is there as He is there," is Buber's translation of Exod. 3:14.

89. *Ibid.*, p. 131.

90. *Ibid.*, p. 135.

91. *Ibid.*, p. 153. Buber translates *middot* as "modes of behavior, fundamental attitudes."

92. *Ibid.*, p. 160.

93. *Ibid.*, p. 130.

94. Buber, *Origin and Meaning*, p. 205.

95. *Ibid.*

96. Buber, *Two Types*, p. 173.

97. *Ibid.*, pp. 173–4, 172.

98. Buber, "Church, State, Nation, Jewry," p. 181.

99. *Ibid.*, p. 179, my emphasis.

100. *Ibid.*, p. 178.

101. Buber, *Israel and the World*, p. 40.

102. Buber, *Two Types*, p. 173. The first part of this suggestion, that Israel should strive for the renewal of its faith through an emphasis on the person, comes as a surprise since there is in this book, as far as I can determine, no direct discussion of how Judaism could benefit from the insights of Christianity. The emphasis throughout is on how *pistis* can come nearer to *emunah*. Because Buber's statement is so radical and so powerfully suggestive, it is also a great disappointment that he does not develop it in any way.

103. Buber, *Israel and the World*, p. 42.

104. *Ibid.*, p. 40, my emphasis.

105. Buber, *Two Types*, p. 12.

106. *Ibid.*, p. 173.

107. Buber, "Church, State, Nation, Jewry," p. 182.

108. Martin Buber, *Two Types*, p. 12, my emphasis.

109. Martin Buber, "Church, State, Nation, Jewry," p. 181.

Chapter Six

1. Mordecai Kaplan, "Martin Buber: Theologian, Philosopher and Prophet," *The Reconstructionist*, 18(May 2, 1952):7.

2. *Ibid.*, p. 8.

3. Mordecai Kaplan, *The Religion of Ethical Nationhood* (New York: The Macmillan Company, 1970), p. 16.

4. Mordecai Kaplan, *Judaism Without Supernaturalism* (New York: The Jewish Reconstructionist Foundation, 1958; The Reconstructionist Press, 1967), pp. 26, 27.

5. On the surface, Kaplan and Buber seem to have much in common: both decry the value of dogma and both extol the values of life-in-community. The similarities, however, are only superficial. Buber, for example, rejects dogma because it is an obstacle to the I-Thou encounter and Kaplan rejects it because it is an obstacle to the pluralism required by a democratic community. Also, for Buber, the belief that the messiah has appeared places one outside of the Jewish tradition. This is not clearly the case for Kaplan, as will become evident later in this chapter. All of these distinctions, of course, stem from differences in their basic orientations: Buber's Judaism is God-centered, Kaplan's is people-centered.

6. Milton Steinberg, quoted by Arnold M. Eisen, *The Chosen People in America, A Study in Jewish Religious Ideology* (Bloomington: Indiana University Press, 1983), p. 94.

7. Kaplan, *Judaism Without Supernaturalism*, p. 207.

8. Indeed, as we shall see, Kaplan accommodates modernity in an extremely uncritical way, going so far as to leave behind questions of truth for questions of expediency.

9. As will be discussed later in this chapter, Kaplan also argues for Jewish existence from a position of cultural pluralism and the belief that all "organic" communities have a right and a will to exist. Kaplan's pragmatic orientation is further reflected in his primary concern for Jewish education and Jewish communal life.

10. Mordecai Kaplan, *Judaism as a Civilization* (1934), (Philadelphia: Jewish Publication Society, 1981), p. 209.

11. Mordecai Kaplan, "We Still Think We are Right: A Reply to a Christian Critic of Reconstructionism," *The Reconstructionist*, 13 (May 2, 1947):15.

12. *Ibid.* Kaplan rejects the traditional notion of salvation as other-worldly bliss, believing it to be unacceptable to modern Jews. He constructs a new notion of salvation that is this-worldly, generally referring to self-fulfillment. But since self-fulfillment is mediated by one's civilization—"It is civilization that spells salvation" for the individual (Kaplan, *Judaism in Transition* [New York: Behrman House, 1941], p. 123)—salvation is closely linked to the survival of the civilization. There are times when Kaplan's use of the term is rather circular: while sometimes salvation is understood as that which supplies the individual with purpose, at other times the individual's purposes are said to constitute his or her salvation (See, for example, Kaplan, *Judaism as a Civilization*, p. 15).

13. Mordecai Kaplan, "The Way I Have Come," in Ira Eisenstein and Eugene Kohn, eds., *Mordecai M. Kaplan, An Evaluation* (New York: The Jewish Reconstructionist Foundation, 1952), p. 302.

14. Kaplan, *Judaism as a Civilization*, p. 182.

15. *Ibid.*, pp. 182-183.

16. *Ibid.*, p. 317. Kaplan offers various descriptions of God, but the overall image is of a "power that makes for salvation." God is not a person but "a quality of universal being, all the relationships, tendencies and agencies which in their totality go to make a human life worthwhile in the deepest and most abiding sense." (Kaplan, *The Meaning of God in Modern Jewish Religion* [New York: Reconstructionist Press, 1955], pp. 25-26.) It is not always clear how God is other than civilization.

17. These quotations offer a good example of the primacy of sociology over theology in Kaplan's thought. Kaplan raises the descriptive level—the way religion *has* functioned in a society—to the normative—the way religion *ought* to function in a society. He ignores data that would argue against his descriptive analysis (the sort of data upon which Buber bases his discussion of religion)—in particular, the place of religion in the lives of mystics, tzadikkim, and prophets, for example. (Buber, on the other hand, hardly deals with the religion of the masses, and his description of the religion of the Hasidim is, according to Gershom Scholem, highly idealized.) By conflating the descriptive with the normative, Kaplan severely skews his picture of Judaism.

18. Kaplan, "The Way," p. 301.

19. Kaplan, *Judaism as a Civilization*, pp. 324, 345.

20. *Ibid.*, p. 345.

21. Kaplan, *Judaism in Transition*, pp. 297-298.

22. Kaplan, *Judaism as a Civilization*, p. 179.

23. *Ibid.*

24. Kaplan criticizes those efforts that reduce Judaism to something less than civilization because he says they cater to the intellectual mood of the time instead of dealing with the true nature of Judaism. And yet it is clear that Kaplan, in seeking for an "idiom" appropriate to his day and in depending upon sociology and psychology to lead him to it, does not escape his own criticism.

25. Kaplan, *Judaism in Transition*, pp. 185 my emphasis, 180.

26. Kaplan, *Judaism as a Civilization*, pp. 180, 184, and elsewhere.

27. *Ibid.*, p. 177.

28. Kaplan, "The Way," pp. 305–306.

29. *Ibid.*, p. 313.

30. *Ibid.*, p. 298.

31. Kaplan, *Judaism as a Civilization*, p. 521.

32. *Ibid.*, p. 336.

33. Kaplan's desire for ecumenism was a major factor in his own unwillingness to declare Reconstructionism to be a new branch of Judaism for many years.

34. Kaplan, "The Way," p. 315.

35. Kaplan, *Judaism as a Civilization*, p. 390.

36. *Ibid.*, p. 319. In accord with Kaplan's "Copernican revolution," it is the people themselves who determine what the sancta will be.

37. *Ibid.*, p. 322.

38. Kaplan does not indicate why or how personal religion would supplement folk religion. Given his understanding of folk religion, it is not clear why personal religion would ever arise and if it did, what use it would serve.

39. Kaplan, *Judaism as a Civilization*, pp. 313, 343.

40. Kaplan defends Reconstructionism against Franklin Littel's charge that the sort of religion Kaplan advocates is similar in many ways to the Volksreligion of the Nazis. (Franklin Littel, "Thoughts About the Future of Christianity and Judaism: A Christian View of Reconstructionism," *The Reconstructionist*, 13(April 4, 1947):10–16 and 13(April 18, 1947):16–22.) Kaplan replies:

> What was wrong with Nazism is not that it sought to invest events and personalities of German history with religious significance, thus creating specifically German *sancta*, but that the Nazis interpreted religion in the narrow national sense which placed the rest of mankind not only outside the circle of salvation, but even outside the circle of the truly human. That they did so may perhaps be attributed to the fact that the universal ideals of Christianity were associated exclusively with *sancta* derived from a foreign source and became equally a victim of Nazi xenophobia. ["We Still Think We are Right," p. 17.]

The "self-consciousness" of one civilization could not be successfully transplanted into the body of another civilization.

41. Kaplan, *Judaism as a Civilization*, p. 320.

42. *Ibid.*, p. 319.

43. Mordecai Kaplan, "The Chosen People Idea as an Anachronism," *The Reconstructionist*, 11(Jan. 11, 1946):17.

44. *Ibid.*

45. Kaplan, *Judaism as a Civilization*, p. 320.

46. Kaplan, "We Still Think We are Right," p. 18; see also Kaplan, *Judaism in Transition*, pp. 272–273.

47. Kaplan, "We Still Think We are Right," p. 19.

48. Kaplan, "Chosen People Idea as Anachronism," p. 20.

49. Kaplan, *Judaism as a Civilization*, p. 399.

50. Kaplan, *Judaism Without Supernaturalism*, p. 34.

51. Arnold Eisen (*The Chosen People in America*, pp. 83–92) notes the interesting relationship between Reform and Reconstructionism on this point: "While Reform accepted chosenness in the form of mission and denied Jewish peoplehood, Kaplan did precisely the opposite. He accepted peoplehood and denied chosenness." [p. 92] However, as Eisen points out, Kaplan affirms a version of chosenness in the form of "vocation," which is finally not unlike the notion of chosenness as reinterpreted by Kaufmann Kohler [p. 83]. In the guise of vocation, writes Eisen, "chosenness, ushered unceremoniously out the front door, was in more modest dress smuggled in through the back" [p. 86]. Nevertheless, I think it can be argued fairly that Kaplan is first and foremost committed to the rejection of chosenness in any of its forms, that the rejection of chosenness is central to his understanding of reality as transnatural and to his formulation of Judaism as a civilization. His advocacy of vocation should be understood as one of the many instances in which Kaplan indulges his pragmatic concerns at the expense of consistency. In contrast to the frequent refrain against chosenness, the concept of vocation is hardly rehearsed, not elaborated, and remains a vague supplement, haphazardly employed. It is for this reason that I have not given attention to "vocation" as an important element in Kaplan's thought.

52. Kaplan, *Judaism Without Supernaturalism*, p. 10.

53. Kaplan, *Judaism as a Civilization*, p. 335.

54. Kaplan, "Chosen People Idea as an Anachronism," p. 13.

55. *Ibid.*, p. 281.

56. *Ibid.*, p. 278. Kaplan's assertions about religious equality follow from his psychological theory; they are not the result of prolonged or careful study of non-Jewish, especially non-Western, traditions.

57. Kaplan, *Judaism as a Civilization*, p. 337.

58. Kaplan, "The Way I Have Come," pp. 319, 318.

59. Mordecai Kaplan, *The Future of the American Jew* (New York: Macmillan, 1948), p. 516.

60. The extent of Kaplan's commitment to civil religion as a necessary and valuable part of national life is evidenced in *The Faith of America* (New York: Henry Schuman, 1951), which he jointly authored with Eugene Kohn and J. Paul Williams, a Christian. Here the American sancta are given the forms of nondenominational prayer, prose, and poetry in a book designed for use on public occasions that call for the celebration of American civilization. It is interesting to note that Kaplan also includes holidays such as Labor Day in the Reconstructionist prayer book.

61. Kaplan, *Judaism as a Civilization*, p. 217.

62. *Ibid.*, p. 216.

63. *Ibid.*, p. 305.

64. Kaplan does not elaborate on the complementary nature of the two civilizations that serve as his primary example, Judaism and Americanism. How do they differ as sources of fulfillment and how do they supplement one another? It is not clear why American civil religion is not sufficiently salvific, especially if its sancta are equivalent to those of Judaism. Kaplan writes that the "loyal religionist who is at the same time a good American will utilize his religious tradition to enrich American culture, and will apply his American experience to enrich the Church tradition that he regards as his own" [*Judaism in Transition*, p. 295] There is mention that Judaism will incorporate the ideals of democracy and that it will in turn be a reminder to American civilization of the "large perspectives" which often elude national groups [*Future of the American Jew*, pp. 516–522]. Moreover, Judaism contributes its "method" to American civilization, a method that "spurns imperialism and that respects individuality" and thus is the key to ethical nationhood ("Judaism and Christianity," *The Menorah Journal* 2(1916):112. This method of Judaism is contrasted with the method of Christianity, which is "imperialism.") But Kaplan does not enter into any sustained discussion of the dynamics involved in coinclusive living, either on an individual or a collective level. Even allowing that Kaplan would not engage in an examination of the theological issues involved, one would expect him to rejoice in this new sociological configuration and spend some time unraveling its implications. That he does not explore the difficulties as well as the possibilities of cultural hyphenism is evidence again that his primary concern is with "what works" or rather with "what seems to be working" and not with why or how something works. Because of his failure to approach these issues with the complexity and depth they require, Kaplan is well-deserving of the serious criticism made by Arnold Eisen (*The Chosen People in America*, p. 97):

> If Passover really was the same as the Fourth of July, in other words, there was no point in Judaism, and the Emperor stood exposed. If the civil religion of America was equal in its saving power to the religion of the Jews, the latter had been trivialized and psychologized without ennobling the former. Jews wanted to be part of America, and yet apart. Kaplan, by pronouncing them an ethnic group and not a faith, set them too far apart, even as, in calling for a shared civil religion, he made them more a part than they wished to be.

65. Kaplan, *Judaism as a Civilization*, p. 419.

66. That someone's "otherness" *is* forfeited in this marital arrangement is not an issue for Kaplan. This is because his argument is primarily a defense of Jewish Americanism and only by implication is he concerned with interfaith relations.

67. Kaplan, *Judaism as a Civilization*, p. 419. Here again Kaplan's reference is to Western civilizations, although he does not make this clarification.

68. *Ibid.*, p. 304.

69. Kaplan, *Judaism in Transition*, p. 305.

70. Kaplan, *Judaism Without Supernaturalism*, p. 199.

71. See, for example, H. R. Niebuhr's suggestions in *The Meaning of Revelation* (New York: Macmillan, 1962).

72. Kaplan, *Judaism as a Civilization*, p. 514.

73. As Eisen points out in regard to Kaplan's god-concept: "We mistake his meaning if we quibble with this or that formulation. The words are not meant to be true. They are meant, rather, to work; to do the job assigned them." [*Chosen People in America*, p. 94]

74. Mordecai Kaplan, "The Chosen People Idea as an Anachronism," p. 17.

75. Mordecai Kaplan, *Judaism as a Civilization*, p. 177.

76. Charles Birch and John B. Cobb, Jr., *Liberation of Life: From the Cell to the Community* (Cambridge: Cambridge University Press, 1985), pp. 183-202.

77. Kaplan, *Judaism as a Civilization*, p. 514.

Chapter Seven

1. Gen. 12:3, Revised Standard Version. The first translation is given in the text. The second translation is given in a note at the bottom of the page.

2. Leo Baeck, *The Essence of Judaism* (N.Y.:Schocken Books, 1961), pp. 222-223.

3. *Ibid.*, pp. 172, 206, 222-23, 251.

4. Martin Buber, "Hasidism in the History of Religions," in *The Origin and Meaning of Hasidism*, ed. and trans. Maurice Friedman (N.Y.: Horizon Press, 1960), pp. 220-239.

5. *Ibid.*, p. 236.

6. *Ibid.*, p. 239.

7. Isaiah Ben-Dasan, *The Japanese and the Jews* (N.Y.: John Weatherhill, 1981), p. 3.

8. Leo Strauss, in his essay, "Progress or Return? The Contemporary Crisis" (*Modern Judaism*, [May 1981]:17-45) argues that the essence of Judaism "is concern with return, it is not a concern with progress." [p. 18] The "progressive man," he argues, lives "unqualifiedly toward the future" and eventually finds himself abandoning Judaism. [p. 19] In contrast is life that is "characterized by the idea of return;" such a life is lived in hopes of a future time when people will be fully faithful to the covenant. Thus while Strauss maintains that "the life of the Jew is the life of recollection," he also holds that "it is at the same time a life of anticipation, of hope." [p. 18] My understanding of Judaism is thus in accord with Strauss on this point: the future *is* "qualified" by the covenant and its promises of redemption.

9. Nolan Pliny Jacobson, *Buddhism and the Contemporary World: Change and Self-Correction* (Carbondale: Southern Illinois University Press, 1983), p. 68.

10. Charles Hartshorne, *Wisdom as Moderation: A Philosophy of the Middle Way* (Albany: State University of New York Press, 1987), p. 54.

11. John B. Cobb, Jr., "Ecology, Ethics, and Theology," in Herman Daly, ed., *Toward a Steady-State Economy* (San Francisco: W. H. Freeman and Co., 1972), pp. 319-320.

12. Irving Greenberg, "Religious Values After the Holocaust: A Jewish View," in Abraham J. Peck, ed., *Jews and Christians After the Holocaust* (Philadelphia: Fortress Press, 1982), p. 76.

13. David Tracy, "Is a Hermeneutics of Religion Possible?" in Leroy S. Rouner, ed., *Religious Pluralism* (University of Notre Dame Press, 1984), p. 129.